Exploring the Andes
and
The Inca Ruins

E G Squier

ISBN: 9781480150263

Folly Cove 01930
Gloucester MA

www.follycove.biz

Table of Contents

OVER THE CORDILLERA.

Equipage for the Cordillara

WHEN, fifteen years ago, I prepared an article on "Ancient Peru," embodying the results of rather extensive investigations among books and manuscripts, I little thought I should ever be able to realize my dream of visiting and exploring the vast region in which was established the largest and best-organized of the aboriginal empires of America, and which was the theatre of the boldest and most dramatic of the Spanish conquests. Yet among Time's changes and accidents came one to me sad and appalling, but which led to the realization of my early dream. Stricken with amaurosis, in the most active and exciting period of our civil war, the light faded away before my eyes, and a dark veil fell slowly between them and the bright and moving world. The skill of the oculist was exerted in vain; every day the darkness deepened, and after some months of ineffectual treatment I was told, kindly but firmly, that further applications were useless, and that perhaps absolute mental rest and a total change of life might reinvigorate the overworked nerves, and restore, in part at least, my failing vision.

A few days afterward, and while suffering under a depression of spirits which only those who have been threatened with blindness can comprehend, I received, from an old and steadfast friend in the Department of State, information of the probable speedy appointment of a mixed commission to sit in Lima "for the settlement of all outstanding claims and points of difference between the United States and Peru," and intimating that my name had been mentioned in connection with the appointment. My ambition to visit the land of the Incas was revived by this intelligence, which created a mental reaction that, no doubt, went far to check the advance of disease. A month later, with my credentials as Commissioner, I was on board a filthy Vanderbilt steamer, bound for the "City of the Kings," as the old, luxurious, licentious capital of Peru was proudly called under the Spanish rule.

At the end of two years, mainly spent in explorations of the country, and during which time I had traveled not far from five thousand miles, crossing and recrossing the Cordillera and the Andes, from the Pacific to the Amazonian rivers, traversing nearly the whole of the great Andean Plateau—the Thibet of America—sleeping in rude Indian huts or on bleak plains in the open air, in hot valleys or among eternal snows, gathering with eager zeal and omnivorous appetite all classes of facts relating to the country, its people, its present and its past—at the end of two years I found myself, surrounded with my trophies of travel, on the deck of a swaying steamer in the harbor of Callao, homeward bound, brown in color, firm in muscle, and with my sight practically restored.

It will require much time, robbed fragmentally from absorbing occupations, and a labor far less stimulating than was spent in collecting my data, to properly prepare them for the public eye; but meantime, perhaps, the readers may not be indisposed to hear something of Peru, its vast interior, its high plains, mighty mountains, and great lakes whose bosoms lie level with the summits of the Alps—as well as of the strange and imposing monuments of human art and ancient greatness which are crumbling away in seacoast valleys, or which, in stony solidity, defy time and the elements on the lofty tablelands of Cuzco and Titicaca. They may be interested to know something of the descendants of the Children of the Sun, whose pride and state rivaled those of Oriental potentates, and whose tragic fate gives to their history the interest of romance. Hardly less interesting will it be to know something of the descendants of the Pizarros and Almagros, and what relations they hold toward the people whose empire they subverted and religion they overthrew—what are their hopes as a nation and their prospects as a republic.

Upon these points something may be learned in the following pages; and without further introduction I ask the reader first to climb with me the mighty Cordillera, into the lofty terrestrial basin of Southern Peru and Bolivia, where repose the silent, enigmatical ruins of Tiahuanaco, the Baalbec of the New World; and then to accompany me to the great lake of Titicaca and its Sacred Islands, whence the Incas dated their origin; and go with me thence, following the footsteps of Manco Capac to Cuzco, the City of the Sun, the capital of the Inca empire, and the Rome of the Western World.

We will pass over the intervening six thousand miles of sea, leave behind us without a word the quaint old city of Panama, through which the tides of emigration have twice flowed —once toward the golden shores of Peru, and again upon the doubly golden strands of California.

Quaint, picturesque Panama, with its ruined temples, vine covered and blossoming walls, slouching negroes, and fruit laden bongos. We will not touch at the emerald islands in its bay, where yellow plantains, russet cocoanuts, and golden oranges, glow out from the eternal green of the trees; nor will we linger at Guayaquil, where the mangroves, like inverted forests, line the slimy shores of its sluggish river, congenial homes of the scaly cayman, and where slumbers sultry and eternal noon. We will not stop for more than a passing glance at the Isla del Muerto, which looks through the yellow haze like some dead giant floating on a drifting plank in the ocean. Nor will we give more than a passing glance at the Island of Puna, where Pizarro bore up so long and faithfully against open foes and treacherous friends, and organized that force wherewith he reduced the grandest, richest, and most powerful of the ancient empires of America.

Coasting along the shores of Ecuador, we may perhaps catch a glimpse of Chimborazo, flaunting its banner of smoke in mid-heaven; but, at any rate, we shall see everywhere a low strip of dingy green, backed by umber colored mountains, and behind them a blue range, tipped here and there with the white of eternal snow. This is the great volcanic range of the Cordillera. By-and-by we turn in toward the land. A cliff of pale gray rock; a narrow beach of pale gray sand; a cluster of pale gray houses, resembling for all the world the nests of the eaves-swallow; with a petty mole, an iron customhouse of pale gray, and a church of the same color; the whole half-defined, and to the stranger appearing to be only a claybank, fantastically worn by the rains. Here we have Paita, the first port in Peru at which touch the steamers of the British South Pacific Mail Steamship Company—a line originated by an American, who had to sell his birthright to England because American capital was too cowardly and too little enterprising to do for America the work Americans ought to do. You will probably go ashore at Yalta, and, with me, traverse the narrow pale gray streets, between the most comical houses of canes and pale gray mud, and mount the pale gray cliffs, and look out listlessly upon the vast plain of pale gray sand, which stretches away twenty leagues to Piura, of which the cluster of huts in Paita is the port. You will be thirsty when you return from this pale gray expedition, and will be told that the water you drink, to wash out your pale gray reminiscences, is brought from a distance of thirty miles on the backs of donkeys. You will not be sorry when you leave Paita, but you will wonder what this portion of burnt-out creation was made for, when the captain tells you that you have seen Peru, or at least its coast, fairly typified in and around Paita, and that for two thousand miles you will find only this dreary waste of barren rock and sand, treeless and lifeless, traversed only here and there, at long intervals, by ribbon-like valleys of green, marking the course of some small stream or river struggling down from the mountains to the sea. Bold men were the conquistadors who coasted slowly along these arid shores in face of the prevailing south wind and against the great Antarctic current. Nothing short of an absorbing love of adventure, and a consuming and quenchless avarice, could have prevented them from putting down their helms and flying shudderingly from the great desolation before them.

Three days from Paita, passing too far from the shore to enable us to see the city of Truxillo, around which spread out the vast ruins of Grand Chimu, we find rising bluff before us, crowned by a lighthouse in the clouds, the bold island of San Lorenzo, inside of which is the harbor of Callao, with its busy huddle of steamers and forest of masts standing out in relief against the yellow walls of the Castle of San Felipe, above whose massive battlements the Spanish flag waved for the last time in Continental America. A noisy crowd of Negroes, Cholos, Chinese, and vagrant fellows of all nations receives us on the mole, where there is a guard of soldiers in red trowsers, and a uniform altogether out-Frenching France, with officers each bearing more golden lace on his person than would fit out a dozen Brigadiers.

Two considerable streams enter the sea near Callao, the Rimac and the Chilion, and their valleys widen out as they approach the ocean, forming a level district of considerable extent, in the centre of which is Lima, the capital of Peru. Behind it rise high, snow capped mountains, among whose topmost peaks are the famous silver mines of Cerro de Pasco. We will not stop to visit Lima now, but leave it and its busy port behind us and continue our course down, or as it is called here, up the coast. For a hundred miles, to the port of Pisco, the shore preserves its aspect of a desert, with the single interruption of the small but wonderfully rich and productive valley of Cañete. At Pisco the stream of the same name comes down to the sea, through a valley literally purple with the grape. Off this valley lie the high, rocky, guano covered islands of the Chinchas, repulsive repositories of treasures richer than the glittering mines of Golconda or Potosi. Beyond Pisco the bare, treeless, silent mountains come close to the sea. I call them mountains, and so they appear to us, but they are only the broken edges of a high desert plateau, undermined by the ocean and corroded by the ceaseless south wind. But one or two streams succeed in penetrating this high desert, and their beds are mere cañons or narrow gorges, with no interval land, and affording no soil nor room for culture. The towns that exist stand back at the foot of the Cordillera, sixty or a hundred miles from the coast, where the streams emerge from the snowy mountains in a full and perennial volume before they are drunk up by the thirsty sands. We touch at but one harbor, as we sail along under the shadow of this desolate tableland, that of Islay, the port of the second city in Peru, Arequipa, ninety miles distant inland, and only to be reached by a forced ride of that length over a desert of shifting sands, in which not a drop of water is to be found nor a blade of grass to be seen. Islay is merely a wretched collection of huts perched on a corroded cliff, full of dark caverns, in which are to be discerned only the flash of the ocean spray, or the gleam of the white wings of the thousands of seabirds which, with multitudes of howling seals, give all there is of life to the shores and islands of Peru.

The great table land of which I have spoken, and along which we sail so closely that its rugged edges shut out from sight the monarch mountains beyond, extends all the way to Arica, the last port but one in Peru, and the principal one in its southern Department of Moquegua, whence we shall start inland on our rough mountain journey.

It is gray morning when our steamer slacks up before the port, and moves slowly to her buoy in the open roadstead. To the right, projecting boldly through the thin mist, half made up of spray from the surf that beats on the rocky shore, and which exaggerates its proportions, we discern the great Morro or headland of Arica. Its face is frayed, seamed, and corroded, and is full of caves and dark, inaccessible grottoes which a Scandinavian imagination would fill with gray, elfin creatures, deformed and malicious, but which our unimaginative glasses show us to be the roosts and refuges of the countless water fowl that flap and shriek around us, and dash up the smooth sea in showers of spray in their eager pursuit of the myriads of fishes that fill these quiet waters. On the very brow of the Morro we detect moving figures, and make out a rude battery, mounted with a few guns, which has been hurriedly erected with a view to intimidate or repel the Spaniards, who have just seized on the Chincha Islands. To the left of the headland there is a low line of verdure, a cluster of modern built houses, a gayly painted church, and a mole—the latter giving us comforting assurance that here we are not to be obliged to perform the difficult feat of landing on the shoulders of a stalwart cholo, staggering over rolling stones through a thundering surf. This is Arica, the port of Tacna, forty miles distant inland in the direction of the snowy Cordillera that lies, in a long line, crowned with frosted silver, high up beyond a great and ominous range of umber colored and treeless mountains. A railway, the longest and almost the only one in Peru, connects Arica with Tacna; and puffs of steam rising fitfully near a long and low, and rather dingy building, indicate the hither terminus of the iron road.

The Port and Morro of Arica

We look inquiringly and with unspeakable interest toward the great mountain billows before us, each succeeding one higher and more mysterious; and wonder what marvels of rock and stream, and what remains of ancient human greatness they conceal; and what will be our own sensations when, after days of travel and toil, and nights of cold and exposure, we shall be swallowed up in their unknown recesses? To one who had read and written of Peru and its wise and powerful Inca rulers, and with whom a journey to the centres of its ancient civilization had been a dream of life, this standing at the portal of the land, and this realization of a wish which had before scarcely assumed more than the outlines of a hope, inspired a feeling of awe and responsibility rather than of eagerness or romance. The vast ranges piled up before me seemed to be barriers interposed by nature against frivolous intrusion.

Let none enter here except with reverence. Seek not to unveil the secrets behind these mighty bars except with humility and truth! Such seemed to be the stern, albeit inarticulate, behest of the great Cordilleras, as on the deck of our swaying steamer I stood face to face with them, rigorous with eternal winter, and severe in their silence and desolation.

Sweeping back from the Morro and behind the town, forming a kind of amphitheatre, is a great wind-row of yellow sand, unrelieved by shrub or blade of grass, on the flanks of which the commandant of the port is drilling his men in evolutions original if not brilliant. This ridge is a huge cemetery of the ancient inhabitants, and is crowded with the desiccated bodies of those who patiently and skillfully cultivated the narrow valley on the borders of which they are buried, or fished from balsas in front of the Morro. Here, as the workmen dug away the sands to fill up the little pier and to open a track for the railway, they found, not alone the poor fisherman wrapped in his own net, and the humble laborer enveloped in braided rushes and stained fabric of cotton, but the more pretentious personage of his day, now equally grim and ghastly, wrapped in a shroud of beaten gold, which rough hands rudely tore away from his dry and crumbling bones, and left them to dissolve in the rasp sea air.

The landing at Arica, as I have intimated, is easy, and a tramway runs from the head of the pier to the custom house to facilitate the transport of goods. On the pier was a pile of coal which had been covered up with matting and rubbish of all kinds, so as to disguise its real character from the Spaniards, who were supposed to be in want of the article and quite likely to use no ceremony in appropriating it if discovered. Other evidence of hostile, or rather defensive intent, was afforded by a succession of rifle pits dug along the shore in front of the town, preparations made under orders of Colonel Prado, Prefect of the Department, who, since, as Dictator of Peru, drove the self same Spaniards ignominiously from the Bay of Callao.

Tacna is high above Arica, not far from 2000 feet; and as the ascent is accomplished in forty miles the grade of the railway is in places very heavy, so that the wheezy locomotive which carries one up travels slowly and painfully. It took us four hours to accomplish the ascent—four hours over a waste of sand loose or indurated, without a semblance of life or verdure, except at the halfway house or station, where there is a subterranean flow of water, and where a few scrubby bushes attest its existence deep in the sands.

The entrance into the valley of Tacna is marked by one of those sudden transitions from desert waste to luxuriance of vegetation which so greatly impresses the traveler in Peru. The azequias, or conduits for irrigation, are always carried as high up on the borders of the valleys as possible, and the water is distributed below, so that the azequia constitutes an abrupt and strongly marked boundary between the barren sands and cultivated fields. These fields, in fact, are as sharply defined as if clipped out with a shears from a sheet of green paper.

We alighted from the train in a very respectable depot, with thrifty piles of merchandise on all sides, just delivered or awaiting transportation, and I handed over unmistakable metal "checks" for my baggage to a man with a cart, who undertook to deliver it at the "Bolo de Oro;" the hostelry whither I had been directed, kept by a Frenchman, and by no means to be confounded with the hotel "Leon de Oro," which is kept by a native, and consequently dirty and uncomfortable. There was quite a gathering around the depot and in the adjacent streets, inasmuch as the day had been set apart for patriotic purposes—that is to say, for listening to denunciations of the Spaniards, for glorifications of Bolivar, and for volunteering. A squad of volunteers were at the depot, quite drunk with enthusiasm and cañaso, and looked as though they would be a useful riddance to Tacna, and would depart amidst ardent aspirations from the entire community that they might all realize the soldier's loftiest ambition, and "die in the arms of victory!"

Tacna has little of the prevailing Oriental aspect of Spanish-American towns. Stone and adobe scarcely enter into the construction of its buildings, which are mostly of wood brought from Chile, from California, or around the Horn, and are run up after the fashion prevalent in our mushroom Western cities. Generally of but one story, the houses of Tacna recall the description of Albany by the rare old geographer Morse: "A city of one thousand houses and ten thousand inhabitants, all standing with their gable ends to the street." The long, low, monotonous lines of gables, with no attempt at architectural relief, are poor substitutes for the heavy arched doorways, Moorish balconies, and jalousies of the older cities, and which, however neglected and tumble down, convey an impression of strength and respectability. Nor is Tacna exceptional in its architecture alone. It has two theatres and but one church.

The Alameda of Tacna

14

The public buildings of Tacna, as I have intimated, are as mean as are its private houses. The only evidence of public spirit is the Alameda, lying quite to one side of the town—a long and rather narrow area, planted with willows, with a broad azequia paved with stones in the middle, and crossed at intervals by stone bridges, modeled after those pictured in Chinese paintings, each surmounted by a coarse marble allegorical statue. There are also stone seats here and there for visitors; but, in common with all the alamedas, or public walks, of the cities of Peru, that of Tacna is the one place above all others deserted. A very fine view is commanded from here of the brown, bare mountains of Pachia, with the snowy peaks of Tacora and Chipicani rising brightly beyond.

My hotel, the Bolo de Oro—I presume it remains the same—was one of the quaintest of caravanseries. The entrance was through the shop of the proprietor, surrounded by shelves gay with bottles of fanciful fashion and labeling, some containing wines and liqueurs, and others comfits and preserves. Every vacant space of wall was covered with chromolithographs of the latest French victories. The hot sunset colors of Solferino and gorgeous tints of Magenta were sufficient to start a perspiration on the coldest day. And then the little round tables sacred to *eau sucré*, cafe, and dominoes! Of French, Frenchy! Not omitting the comfortable looking *Madame la Propriétaire*, who sat at her sewing behind the counter, and dispensed smiles, bonbons, *bon mots*, absinthe, and cigars with equal alacrity and grace. Behind the shop was, of course, the inevitable billard, opening on a court set round closely with little wooden buildings, resembling on a slightly exaggerated scale those sold in the toy shops, and all presenting their gables to the court. Each gable was penetrated by a door, and over the door was a window hung on a pivot, opened and shut by a cord inside, which afforded light and air to the interior—a single room, with a cot, a small table, a smaller washstand, a single chair, and a tall candle. From the further end of the court rises a perennial fragrance of onions, and there is a gentle and constant sizzling of frying meats, appetizing enough, but suffering some detraction from the circumstance that the way to the closets is through the kitchen, dirty as French kitchens always are, and which are clean only by comparison with the Spanish.

Bolivia has only one port on the Pacific, Cobija, 300 miles south of Arica; but as the road thence to La Paz, the capital, is long and difficult, over a region indescribably desolate, communication between the coast and the interior is chiefly carried on, as I have already said, through Tacna, which is the true *entrépot*, not of Bolivia alone, but of the larger part of the important Peruvian department of Puno. It would be supposed, therefore, that ample facilities exist in Tacna for the journey inland, and that no difficulty would be encountered in obtaining the supplies and equipments necessary for it. I was assured in Lima that "everything" could be had in Tacna; but, happily, was too old a traveler to neglect making some provision for the trip. Happily, I say, for it was with the greatest difficulty I could obtain the cooking utensils, pans, kettles, coffee pots, and other requisites for travel in an uninhabited region, or among a people ignorant of the appliances of civilization. After long search I found a broken *cafetéra*, in which alcohol could be used for boiling coffee. This I repaired with my own hands, after the job had been given up by the clumsy native tinman as impossible; and it proved to be my best friend on many an occasion when neither wood nor other material for lighting a fire or heating water was to be found, sometimes for days together. The hammock—that supremest device for human rest, repose, and enjoyment, afternoon siesta or midnight slumber, the solace and reliance of the traveler in Central America and Mexico, in which he may suspend himself in happy security above the filth of his dormitory, and out of the reach of its vermin—is useless among the sierras of Peru. There are no trees between which to swing it in the uninhabited regions, and the mud and stone huts of the Indians and *lomeros*, besides being generally too low, afford no projections to which it may be fastened. Unless, therefore, the traveler has made up his mind to rough it in roughest fashion, wrapped only in his blanket at night, or to take the risk of finding now and then a filthy sheepskin for his couch, he must literally carry his bed with him—a necessity imposed also by the severe cold of the interior. So I had a mattress made in Tacna, light and handy, covered with leather on the under side to prevent the absorption of damp from the ground, and as a protection, when rolled up and on the mule's back, against the rain—a brilliant device, on which I never ceased to congratulate myself, and which saved me, no doubt, from indefinite rheumatism, not to say something worse. It took five days to get my mattress made. I had to buy the wool in one place, the ticking in another, the leather elsewhere, and when I had collected all these, the dusky individual who condescended to put them together demanded, in a tone equally reproachful and imperious, "But where are the needles and the thread?" I acknowledged my oversight, apologized in fact, and proceeded to obtain them. I only wonder now that the mattress maker of Tacna allowed me to keep on my hat in his august presence.

There is, of course, but one mode of reaching the interior from Tacna, and that is on mule back. But to obtain mules is both difficult and expensive. I had been recommended to an arriero named Berrios, who had had the honor of conducting that extraordinary superfluity of our diplomatic establishment, the American Minister to Bolivia, over the Cordillera, and who had also accompanied Mr. Forbes in his geological explorations, and in his ineffectual attempt to reach the as yet untrodden summit of Tacora. But Berrios looked yellow and ill, and complained that two nights among the snows of Tacora had nearly finished him. Besides, his mules had not had time to recover from the fatigues of their last trip over the mountains two months before. Furthermore, they were at pasture in the valley of Lluta, fourteen leagues distant, beyond the desert. Finally, however, after much diplomatizing and a great concentration of mercantile influence, to say nothing of the offer of about double the usual rate of hire, Berrios undertook to supply me with mules, and to accompany me himself, aided by two mozos, all the way to Puno. After having fixed the day two or three times, and as often disappointed me, the echoes of the patio of the Bolo de Oro were startled one afternoon by the clatter of hoofs, the jingling of spurs, and a general rush of a dozen mules, which hustled in before the cracking whips of Berrios and his mozos. We were to have started at daylight, and slept at Palca, the last aldea, or village, before finally plunging among the mountains and entering on the Despoblado. But now we could get no farther than Pachia, three leagues distant. Having been waiting, booted and spurred, since dawn, I was not in the best of humor; and my ruffled temper was by no means soothed on discovering two mules already loaded with baggage not my own, and learning that it belonged to a party of three Bolivians, who had arranged with Berrios for the mountain trip subsequently to his engagement with me. It was to suit their convenience that I had been detained in Tacna; and they had, moreover, already gone on to Pachia, where they would, no doubt, monopolize the limited accommodations of the little tambo at that place.

I confess to a decided liking for mules—not less for their patience, sure footedness, and faithful service than for their little wicked ways. The cargo mule thinks that every moment his load can be evaded is an hour of happiness gained; and although, when it is once on his back, he will walk off resigned, if not perfectly content, he will resort to every expedient his thick head is capable of devising to avoid receiving it. It was amusing to see Berrios and his mozos chase around the patio after a mule that would dodge in and out among its fellows until cornered, and then lay back its ears, put its nose to the ground, and kick out with vicious vehemence, until the lasso was once around its neck, when it would surrender itself tamely, and receive its load with expression of face as gentle and demure as if it rejoiced in its lot, and had years before repented of all mulishness. There was one, however, the largest and most powerful of the lot, who held out to the last; and nothing could be done with him until a poncho was thrown over his head and tied under his throat, leaving only his nose uncovered. But the spite and malice that quivered in the withdrawn upper lip, and glanced from his broad, yellow teeth, and nestled in every wrinkle, when the girths were tightened by two men surging on each side, with one foot braced against his ribs, were past description. He became quiet enough, however, long before we got to Puno, and as humble as the rest.

A traveler accoutred for a journey among the Andes is a picturesque if not an imposing personage. Heavily clothed and booted, with a felt hat with a broad brim, capable of being bound down over his ears for the double purpose of warmth and security against being blown away by the currents of wind that suck through narrow gorges or sweep over unsheltered heights with hurricane force, his neck wound round with a gayly colored bufanda, a thick, native made poncho of vicuña or llama wool over his shoulders, and falling to his knees, a serviceable knife stuck in his bootleg, spurs that look like cart wheels minus their perimeters, and not much smaller, which jangle as he treads and tinkle as he rides, a rifle hanging at the bow of his saddle, and a well filled alforgas fastened behind him—these go to make up the equipment of the adventurer among the mountains; that is to say, if he have what the Spaniards call *sabiduria*, and we call gumption. It only requires the addition of a large pair of green goggles to protect the eyes from the glare of sun and snow, to make one's best friend irrecognizable.

The road from Tacna to Pachia lies straight across the sandy desert, into which the traveler enters soon after leaving the town, while the narrow, cultivable valley deflects in a curve to the right. The distance is ten miles, and the rise 1630 feet, but scarcely perceptible to the eye, probably from being regular and constant. It was dark when we reached the tambo—a collection of mere huts, but for default of a better place a resort of the *jeunesse* of Tacna, who gallop out here to eat dulces, drink chicha, fight cocks, and in other modes gratify the universal Spanish passion for play. As I had anticipated, the intruding Bolivians were already on the spot, and had taken possession of the mud banks that ran around the solitary apartment of the tambo, and which, throughout the interior, are the sole substitutes for bedsteads. Some young foreigners, however, out for a holiday, who had a kind of clubhouse or club hut close by the tambo, invited me to share it and their supper with them, which I was glad to do; and I was especially pleased to observe my Bolivians still hungry after their meal of sloppy chupe, sneaking around the door of our hut, and glancing with longing eyes at our table on which were heaped the edibles of three continents.

And as chupe is the eternal and almost always the sole dish obtainable in the interior of Peru and in Bolivia, I may as well dispose of it at once. It may be described as a kind of watery stew, which on the coast and in the principal towns is made up of vegetables and fragments of different kinds of meat and fish, boiled together and seasoned with salt and aji or peppers, and is sometimes rather savory, or at least eatable. As we go into the interior it decreases in richness as the materials for making it become fewer and tougher, until it consists of only a few square pieces of lean mutton and some small, hard, bitter, water soaked potatoes, floating about in a basin of tepid water, which at most has simmered a little over a smouldering fire of llama or cow's dung, from the smoke of which it has absorbed its predominant flavor. A little brown salt from the native salt quarries, in which it is mixed with a variety of other and astringent ingredients, constitutes the only seasoning. One wonders how life can be kept up in these frigid regions on such thin and unsubstantial fare. Unhappy is the traveler here who has not made provision for the frequent occasions when nothing but the most diluted chupe can be obtained, and for the not infrequent occasions when not even this poor substitute for food can be procured. Detesting it in its best form I literally loathed it in its degeneracy, and only ate it with inexpressible stomachic protests.

We left Pachia at three o'clock in the morning. The air was chill, and we already experienced the usefulness of our thick ponchos. Our cavalcade was strung out in a long line, and as we followed each other silently over the echoless sand, we might have been mistaken for a ghostly procession. When day dawned we found ourselves already hemmed in by the steep slopes of the Quebrada de la Angostura, through which descends, with a rapid current and many a leap and bound, one of the brawling affluents of the stream that fructifies the oasis of Tacna. A few dwarf molle trees, which somewhat resemble our willows, but which bear a berry in taste much like that of our red cedar, found scant foothold here and there along the stream, far below our narrow path, which was little more than a shelf worn in the abrupt hillside by the tread of countless mules and llamas. The ascent was steep, and the gorge narrow and barren for two leagues, when we came to a point where the quebrada widens out into something like a valley. Just before entering this valley, at the right of the mule path, we came upon a rock or boulder covered with figures, which Barrios pointed out to me as a rare relic of antiquity. Roughly pecked in the rock, barely penetrating its ferruginous crust, I observed a great number of circles and semicircles, some angular figures, and rude representations of llamas, mules, and horses. The latter appeared no fresher or later than the former, and all looked as if they might have been worked in the stone yesterday by the same idle and unskillful hand.

In the narrow valley, which now takes the name of the Quebrada de Palca, there were many desperate attempts at cultivation, particularly of lucerne, always in great demand as fodder for the mules entering the Despoblado, and Berrios bought here a little and there a little there was not much in all—which was packed on the sumpter horse and the lightly laden mules, and behind the albardas of the mozos. It was a wise provision of Berrios, as we found out afterward.

At eleven o'clock A.M. we came in sight of Palca, a poor but picturesque little caserio or village, with a small white church gleaming out against the dull brown of the bare mountain side. The village is five leagues from Pachia, and 9700 feet above the sea. There were some scant fields of maize and lucerne around it, and the lower slopes of the mountains were thinly sprinkled with stems of the columnar cactus. Here and there in the valley, standing on little natural knolls or artificial eminences, we saw a number of ancient burial towers, which afterward became familiar to us under the name of chulpas. They are rectangular in plan, from six to ten feet square at the base, slightly widening upward, and from ten to fifteen feet high.

Beyond Palca the quebrada narrows again, and the path was at one time high up on the slopes of the mountains, at a dizzy height above the fretting torrent below, and next in the very bed of the rapid, stony stream, not unfrequently between rocks almost closing above our heads, giving to the atmosphere a chill, sepulchral feel that made us shiver beneath our heavy ponchos. Here we began to meet atajos, or trains of mules, descending from the resting place or dépot of La Portada, laden with bags of barilla (copper, or tin ore), which is brought to that point by llamas. These atajos are always led by an educated horse with a sonorous bell attached to his neck to warn approaching travelers to stop at some spot where the road is wide enough to prevent their being run down outright or toppled over the precipices by the thundering, heavily laden train that plunges down behind the equine leader. The fear of being thus run down is what most disturbs the traveler in the Sierra, where there are many long and dangerous passes, with paths so narrow as not to admit of two animals passing each other. It is customary to shout or to blow a shrill blast on a pandean pipe, which every arriero carries for this purpose, before entering on these dangerous sections of road, which is responded to by whoever happens to be struggling along it. If not answered the road is supposed to be clear.

We passed several great stacks of bags of barilla as we went on, and one or two storehouses of corrugated and galvanized iron for receiving ores, and, still ascending, came to a little open space, where, on the shelves of the steeps around us, we observed a number of burial towers similar to those which we had noticed, two leagues below, at Palca. I dismounted to examine them, and ran a thorn or spine of the cactus into my foot, through the thick leather of my boot, in my eagerness to reach them, which it took half an hour to extract.

Chulpa or Burial Tower

Primarily these chulpas consisted of a cist or excavation in the ground, about four feet deep and three feet in diameter, walled up with rough stones. A rude arch of converging and overlapping stones, filled in or cemented together with clay, was raised over this cist, with an opening barely large enough to admit the body of a man, on a level with the surface of the ground, toward the east. Over this hollow cone was raised a solid mass of clay and stones, which, in the particular chulpa I am now describing as a type of the whole, was sixteen feet high, rectangular in plan, seven and a half feet face by six feet on the sides. The surface had been "rough cast" with clay, and over this was a layer of finer and more tenacious clay or stucco, presenting a smooth and even surface. At the height of fourteen feet was a cornice or projection of four inches, and of about six inches in vertical thickness, formed by a layer of compacted ichu or coarse mountain grass, placed horizontally, and cut off evenly as by a shears. Above this the body of the chulpa reappeared, a little frayed by time and weather, to the height of about eighteen inches.

The whole structure rested on a square or rather rectangular platform of roughly hewn stones, extending about four feet around it on every side.

The stuccoed surface of the chulpa had been painted in white and red, as shown in the engraving, where the shaded parts represent the red, and the light parts the white of the original. The opening, as before stated, was toward the east, on a level with the platform, and was about eighteen inches wide and high. But every other face of the chulpa had a painted opening, which led me to think that the real one had once been closed and also painted over, so that the fronts corresponded in appearance. However that may be, I wedged myself through the opening into the cist or vault, the bottom of which was covered a foot deep with human bones and fragments of pottery. There were no entire skulls, but many fragments of skulls in the cist —a circumstance by no means surprising, as these remains are close by a principal road or trail from the coast to the interior, which has been more or less traversed by curious and Vandalic people for three hundred years.

Although I did not obtain a skull from these chulpas I secured one from another point, a few leagues distant, of which I give an engraving. It is a fine specimen of the Aymara skull, artificially distorted and lengthened.

At the chulpas our mules had begun to pant and stagger under the influence of the soroche, or rarefaction of the air, but which Berrios insisted was from the vets, or influence due to mineral substances (vetas or veins of metal) in the earth. And, in reality, at a little distance farther on, although meanwhile our ascent had been constant, they seemed to have sensibly recovered, but still showed signs of the soroche.

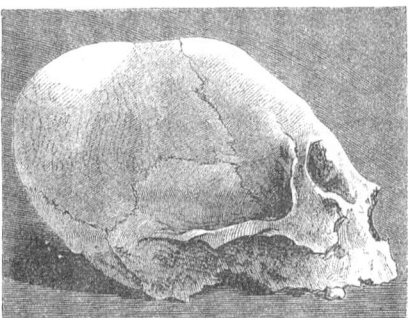

Aymara Skull from Totora

At three o'clock we turned abruptly from the gorge of the torrent, which we had been following, now reduced to a trickling rivulet, and began to climb the steep mountainside on our right, zig-zagging towards the cumbre or crest. Two hours were occupied in this slow and painful ascent, the mules suffering much, and frequently stopping to recover breath. From the summit of the ridge—which was the divide between two of the sources of the Rio de Tacna—although bleak mountains still rose above us, cutting off from view the still higher Nevadas, or snowy mountains beyond them, we could, nevertheless, look down with scarce an interruption on the great sandy plateau of the coast, in which the valley of Tacna appeared only as a speck. A thin white, but confusing, haze cut off our view of the ocean; but the intervening desert, dull and monotonous, was clearly defined.

On what may be termed the saddle of the crest are the remains of tambos, or stone edifices, which the provident Incas had erected as hospices or refuges for the travelers between the coast and the interior. So called Spanish civilization has supplied nothing of the kind, albeit, as I have said, this is the principal route of travel and commerce between the capital of Bolivia and the sea.

Descending from this ridge we found ourselves in another gorge or valley somewhat wider than that by which we ascended, and watered by a larger stream. Following up this, it being now late in the afternoon, we began to experience the cold consequent on our great altitude, and became aware of an unnatural distension of our lips and swelling of our hands, due to diminished atmospheric pressure. Icicles depended from the dripping rocks in shaded places, and the pools of the stream were bridged over with ice. Suddenly we came to a point where the rocks closed so nearly as to permit but one loaded animal to pass at a time, stumbling through the stream among loose stones and the skeletons of mules—a dark, cold, shuddering place! Fortunately the pass, which is that of La Portada (the portal), is not long, and we soon emerged from it, in sight of the great corral and depository of barilla, of the same name, standing upon a kind of shelf on the mountainside, with the stream chafing close to it on the left.

The merchants of Tacna have built here a rude inclosure for the droves of llamas that come from the interior with products for the coast, and here also is a little cluster of buildings for persons connected with the trade—homely and poor, but a welcome refuge for the tired traveler. As we rode up a troop of more than a thousand llamas, with proudly curved necks, erect heads, great, inquiring, timid eyes, and suspicious ears thrust forward as if to catch the faintest sound of danger, each with its hundred pounds of ore secured in sacks on its back, led, not driven, by quaintly costumed Indians, filed past us into the inclosure of the establishment.

We obtained hospitality in one of the buildings of La Portada. But let not my readers mistake the meaning of the word hospitality. In Peru it consists generally in permitting you, with more or less of condescension, to spread your own bed on the mud floor of an unswept room, alive with vermin, with a single rickety table for its chief and often its only article of furniture. It consists in permitting you to cook your own food, with fuel for which you will not be obliged to pay your host or his servant acting under his direction, much more than four times its value, and who expects that you will permit him to take the lion's share of your preserved meats, and no inconsiderable portion of your last bottle of the stimulant you most affect, which can not be replaced, and which is here often vitally necessary.

I have crossed the Alps by the routes of the Simplon, the Grand St. Bernard, and St. Gothard, but at no point on any of them have I witnessed a scene so wild and utterly desolate as that which spreads out around La Portada. There is neither tree nor shrub; the frosty soil cherishes no grass, and the very lichens find scant hold on the bare rocks. In altitude La Portada is 12,600 feet above the sea, or about 1000 feet higher than the hospice of the Grand St. Bernard, and but little lower than the untrodden summit of the Eiger. The night was bitterly cold. The cañaso aguardiente, or native rum, which I had purchased for making coffee in my cafetéra, refused to burn, and extinguished the lighted match thrust into it as if it were water. I was obliged to abstract some refined alcohol from my photographic stores to supply its place, with which my Bolivian companions made themselves free, besides taking the best places for their beds, and leaving only the table and a narrow bench for H— and myself.

The Nevados of Tacora and Chipigani from the Pass of Guaylillos

Before going to bed I went out to the corral. The llamas had been fed each with a handful of maize, and were crouching on their bellies, with their legs mysteriously folded beneath their fleeces and invisible, but with their heads erect, and ears thrust forward, chewing their cuds with an expression of distant contemplation such as we often observe in confirmed smokers. If I were to paint a picture of rest it would not be of a child in slumber, of a Hercules leaning on his club, nor yet of a harvester reclining beside his sheaves, but of a llama in repose. The group impressed me in the starlight as the sphinxes did when looking up the lane of Luxor. The Indians who had charge of the llamas had built up a semicircular wall against the wind with bags of barilla, and had lighted a smouldering fire of taquia, or llama dung, thrusting into it from time to time fragments of meat, which they ate from their fingers, while their poor dish of chupe seethed and simmered over the unfragrant embers. They were as silent and abstracted as the animals they attended, and took no apparent heed of what went on around them.

We were in the saddle at dawn and resumed our upward path. The road was narrow and slippery, for every spring, rivulet, and pool of water was frozen solid. The murmur of the stream that flowed past La Portada was hushed beneath its icy armor. At eight o'clock we seemed to be close on the cumbre, but it was nine o'clock before the silver peaks of Tacora and Chipicani began to show themselves, and the sun to stream into our faces from the east —a genial and welcome apparition.

Half an hour later, our mules laboring severely and stopping momentarily to recover breath, we reached the Pass of Guaylillos, marked, as is every other high pass in Peru, by an apacheta, or great cairn, raised by the Indians, each one of whom as he passes adds a stone on it or a quid of coca, as an offering or propitiation to the genius of the mountain, who has the power of conferring strength and relieving fatigue. This apacheta is about twenty feet high, surmounted by a rude cross, and with its slopes covered with the skeletons and desiccated bodies of mules that had here succumbed under the influence of the soroche.

The Pass of Guaylillos is 14,750 feet above the sea, or but little less than the altitude of Mount Blanc, and more than double that of Mount Washington. The view backward from this point presents only a series of dark brown, desolate ridges radiating toward the sea, the buttresses of the high, broken plain in front, bristling with snowy peaks, from some of which may be seen issuing plumes of smoke, indicating their volcanic character. Between us and the icy Tacora and Chipicani, rising 8000 feet above our heads, their pure summits yet untouched by human foot, is a broad but shallow valley covered with hardy puna grass, now sere and withered, but affording food for a flock of graceful vicuñas, which lift high their heads and stare straight at us as I fire my rifle, the report of which sounds wonderfully hollow and weak in the thin atmosphere. While we sat gazing on this grand but bleak and wintry scene, the distended nostrils and heaving sides of our animals telling painfully how great was their difficulty in breathing, we were startled by the sudden fall from his saddle of one of our Bolivian companions under the effects of the soroche. On lifting him from the ground we found him nearly senseless, with blood trickling from his mouth, ears, nostrils, and the corners of his eyes. Copious vomiting followed, and we administered the usual restoratives with good effect. In doing this I drew off my gloves, and was surprised to find my hands swollen and covered with blood which appeared as if it had oozed from a thousand minute punctures. Excepting this, a tumefaction of the lips, and occasionally a slight giddiness, I did not suffer from the rarefaction of the air or from the vets while in the interior of Peru, although for six months I was seldom less than 13,000 and often as high as 18,000 feet above the sea.

We wound down by an easy path into the valley that intervened between us and the base of Tacora, at the bottom of which we came to the Rio de Azufre. Its banks, as its name implies, are yellow and orange with sulphurous deposits, and lined with the skeletons of horses, mules, and llamas that had ventured to drink its poisonous waters. I tasted the water, and found it abominably acrid and bitter. Indeed, all the water of the Despoblado, even that which to the taste does not betray any evidence of foreign or mineral substances in solution, is more or less purgative, and often productive of very bad effects. In many parts of the country the thirsty traveler discovers springs as limpid and bright as those of our New England hills; yet when he dismounts to drink, his muleteer will rush forward in affright with the warning cry, "Beware; es aqua de Veruga!" The Veruga water is said to produce a terrible disease, called by the same name, which manifests itself outwardly in both men and animals in great bleeding boils or carbuncles, which occasion great distress and often result in death.

From the Rio de Azufre our path wound round the base of Tacora, which is of volcanic origin, and 22,687 feet in elevation, and gradually ascended to a broad plain, sloping gently to the right, covered with stones, sere ichu grass, and clumps of a low resinous shrub called tola. Groups of vicuñas were scattered over the plain, and at a low, marshy spot, near where a patch of ground white with the effloresence of some kind of salts showed the existence of a shallow pool in the season of rains, we observed a belt of light green grass, on which a troop of llamas was feeding. They were interspersed with vicuñas, which grazed by their side as if members of the same community.

I need not say that we were eager to get a shot at the vicuñas, but they were shy, and kept well out of reach. I dismounted, and endeavored to steal from one clump of bushes, and from one rock to another, until within reasonable range; but always at the critical moment the male of the family—they always run in groups of ten or a dozen, females and young ones, under the lead of a single patriarch — would stamp his foot and utter a strange sound, half-neigh half-whistle, and, away they would dart with the speed of the wind, only, however, to stop at a safe distance and stare at us intently, not to say derisively. After several attempts and failures I ventured a random shot at a group fully half a mile distant. They bounded away, all but one, which after going a few yards stopped short. "Es herido es herido!" —he is wounded! he is wounded!—shouted my companions, who threw off their ponchos and alforgas, and calling to me to follow their example, started on a chase after the wounded animal. And such a chase I venture to say was never before seen at the foot of solemn old Tacora! The shot had broken one of the forelegs of the vicuña, just below the knee, but we soon found that with his three sound legs he was more than a match for us, on a stern chase. After half an hour's hard riding we stopped to arrange a little piece of strategy, and the vicuña stopped also, as if to say, "Take your time, gentlemen I am a little sore, but in no kind of a hurry!" Our plan was soon fixed, and we separated, making long detours so, as to surround our victim, whom we were to dispatch with our revolvers as he attempted to break through our line. He regarded the whole proceeding with complacency, and never moved, except to contemplate us one after another as we closed slowly and cautiously around him. Nearer and nearer, and still he never moved. We were almost within pistol range, and our fingers were already on our triggers, when with a bound he dashed between me and Berrios, who had joined in the chase, with the velocity of an arrow. I fired twice rapidly, and Berrios discharged his rusty horse pistol, loaded with a half-pint of slugs, without effect, when our excited Bolivians, closing in, commenced an irregular fusillade, sending their bullets singing around us in most unwelcome proximity. I suspect I came much nearer being shot than the vicuña, and not choosing to take more risks gave up the chase. But the Bolivians kept on, while Barrios, H—, and myself toiled back to the mule path and onward to the tambo of Tacora.

Nevada and Tambo of Tacora

This tambo, which is a favorable type of what in Switzerland would be called "refuges," consists of four low buildings of stones and mud, thatched with ichu, and surrounding a small court, in which the travelers' animals are gathered at night. Sometimes, and for the accommodation of the troops of llamas, there is a large supplementary corral, or inclosure, constructed of loose stones, or stones laid in mud. Often these tambos are without keepers, occupants, or furniture of any kind; but that of Tacora had a resident, who occupied the principal building, in which he had a scant store of wilted alfalfa, or lucerne, and a few articles of food, principally the flesh of the vicuña. Another building served as a kitchen; a third for the storage of cargo and as a dormitory for the arrieros; while the fourth was reserved for travelers. It had no entrance or opening except the doorway, elevated two feet above the ground, and barely large enough to permit a full grown person to squeeze through. This was closed with a flap of raw hide. The interior was dark and dirty beyond description. I doubt if it had been swept, or if any attempt had been made to cleanse it, for many months. It had no furniture whatever, only there was the usual mud bank on every side of this den whereon the traveler might spread his bed.

The keeper of the tambo, wearing a slouched felt hat, and wrapped in a blue cloak with a fur collar and a gilt clasp at the neck as big as one's hand, complied loftily and somewhat haughtily with our request for some cebada, or barley, for our mules; and motioned to one of his Indian women to cook some chupe for our mozos. We preferred to open a can of stewed beef and a box of sardines for our dinner. I observed that the proceeding arrested the attention of our distant host, with whom we had signally failed to open conversation, but who now seemed to have been suddenly called down from his contemplations to a cognizance of what was going on around him. I think I never saw a more fixed and eager gaze than that he fastened on our edibles and on our bottle of brandy. His eyes followed every morsel from the plate to our mouths with an expression of indescribable longing. There was no evading the conclusion that the man was ravenously hungry, but if there had been any doubt, the alacrity with which he responded to my invitation to join us, and the unctuous "como no?"—"why not?" of his reply would have dispelled it. He certainly did justice to his meal, if not to us, for he made no pause until the last morsel had disappeared, which it did just as our Bolivians came in, panting and exhausted, from their fruitless chase after the wounded vicuña. I could not resist encroaching a little on my stores, under the circumstances, in their behalf, and gave them also a can of beef and a box of sardines. Our host did not wait to be invited to join them, and when I left the tambo for a ramble in its neighborhood I observed that the larger part of this feast also was disappearing behind the wonderful gilt clasp. But all this did not prevent him from demanding a price for his cebada and chupe which made Berrios speechless with astonishment.

Beyond the tambo the ground becomes a little undulating and broken, but soon subsides into a broad plain white with efflorescence of some kind, at the lower part of which appeared La Laguna Blanca, a considerable but apparently shallow sheet of water, along the edges of which we discerned vast numbers of waterfowl. Several mountain streams, fed from the snows, descending from the slopes on our left, had taken the mule track for their channel, and we splashed along for a mile or more through the icy water. The plain now became less stony, and more thickly overgrown with tola. Vicuñas, too, were more numerous and less shy, and toward evening we were able to approach so near them that I might have shot a dozen, if I liked, with my revolver. We contented ourselves with one, taking with us only the saddle, and leaving the rest to the condors.

The ground over which we rode during the afternoon, and after leaving La Laguna Blanca behind us, rose gently in a broad swell or billow, which here, although nearly a thousand feet lower than the ridge of Guaylillos, is the real divide, separating the waters flowing into the Pacific from those discharging into the lakes of the great terrestrial basin of Titicaca. From its summit a fine view is obtained, stretching southward to an immense distance, with the smoking cones of the undescribed volcanoes of Pomarope and Sahama on the horizon.

At the foot of this dividing ridge we come to the considerable, clear, and rapid stream of Uchusuma, flowing into the Rio Maure, which in turn falls into the Desaguadero, or outlet of Lake Titicaca, itself pouring its flood into the unmapped and mysterious lake of Aullagas.

The Casitas of Uchusuma

Night began to close around us soon after passing the river, and we turned abruptly to our right, across the tolares, or tola fields, into a shallow valley near the stream, where Berrios said there was some grass for the animals, and some casitas for ourselves. We soon reached a little group of low stone huts, hardly bigger than the houses the beaver builds, and quite as rude. They had been erected by a couple of Indian families, who undertook to pasture a drove of llamas on the banks of the Uchusuma, but who had all died of smallpox about two years before our visit. The casitas had fallen rapidly into ruin. The wind had torn great holes through the thatch of the roofs, and the frost had made breaches in the rough walls. Our Bolivians, who always contrived to get in ahead of us, took hasty possession of the best preserved and largest of the huts, and we were fain to take the next best, which had been the chapel. It was not an imposing structure, the interior being barely seven feet long by five feet wide, and so low as to prevent a man of ordinary height from standing erect. At the further end was a little altar of mud, and a little wooden cross hung undisturbed against the rough stonewall. There

33

was barely room to stow away our saddles and alforgas, and spread our two beds. We closed the orifice which answered for a door with a blanket, and then set about cooking our saddle of vicuña. All hands turned out to gather the dry stems and roots of the Iola, which burn fiercely and rapidly, and we soon had a bright fire blazing in one of the half-unroofed huts, which we had improvised as a kitchen. Our baggage was arranged in a square, and a tarpaulin spread over all, forming a sort of tent, which here and subsequently was the sole protection of Berrios and the mozos, and which we were often too glad to share with them.

I can't say much for vicuña flesh on first trial and when freshly killed, and would prefer good mutton to it at any time. We nevertheless had chupe of vicuña, and vicuña steaks, and might have had a joint of vicuña, if we could have had a fire constant enough to roast it by. On the whole I don't think I had a good appetite that night, and fell back early on coffee, the traveler's best reliance under all circumstances and in every clime.

Our dormitory at Uchusuma

We had burned out the last stem of our supply of tola before we stole to our couches in the chapel. The sky was dark as a pall, and the stars burned out on the still, bitter air with unnatural lustre. I watched them through the openings in the roof of our rude dormitory until midnight, and then fell asleep and dreamed that they were golden tipped spears, darting down from the sky. Berrios did not rouse us early next morning, not until the sun was up, for every one was cold and stiff and needed thawing out. My beard was matted with ice, and the blanket around my head was spangled over with the frost.

We were now fairly entered on the cold, arid region known as the Despoblado, that dreary, desolate, silent region, which forms the broad summit of the Cordillera. It has the aspect of an irregular plain, and is diversified with mountain ridges and snowy and volcanic peaks, imposing in their proportions, notwithstanding that they rise from a level 14,000 feet above the sea. In all directions spread out vast tolares or tola fields, with here and there patches of ichu grass, which grows in clumps, and at this season is dry and gray, stiff and needle-like. Toward noon we came to many broad dry runways or channels, between disrupted beds of trachytes, and indicating that, during the rainy season, heavy volumes of water descend from the Aucomarca and Quenuta mountains and ranges to the north. Just at noon we reached the Rio Caño, a rather broad and shallow stream, flowing in a sandy bed, and which is here the boundary between Peru and Bolivia. On its opposite bank rises a cliff of porphyry, fissured and broken in a thousand shapes, which deflected our path to the southward until we reached a point of practicable ascent for animals.

Among the rocks we saw for the first time the biscacha, about the only quadruped, except those of the llama family, that is found in the Altos of Peru. It is of the chinchilla family, about the size and shape of a rabbit, gray on the back, reddish brown on the belly, but with a long tail like that of the squirrel, which it curves up over its back in sitting erect, as is its custom, like the latter animal. It has some of the quaint and amusing habits of the prairie dog of our own country, and delights to perch itself on some point of rock, whence it will contemplate the traveler silently and without motion, only, however, to plunge down suddenly into some covert with the quickness of light; but as often without as with apparent reason. After a few moments absence he will very likely appear again, first projecting his head above the rocks, then his shoulders, and, should the reconnoissance prove satisfactory, he will resume his erect position, perhaps, however, to repeat his previous gymnastic feat a second after. The biscacha is esteemed good food, provided the tail is cut off immediately after it is killed. If this is not done the natives maintain the animal is corrumpido. For myself I class the flesh of the biscacha with that of the vicuña as a possible alternative against starvation.

An hour later, some very regular elevations or table rocks appearing on our right in the distance, we came to the Rio Maure, a large stream flowing in a deep channel between high cliffs of purple porphyry-conglomerate, which is here fissured and weather worn into a thousand castellated and fantastic shapes. The descent to the water is by a steep, breakneck path, partly worn and partly worked among the rocks, and down which it seems incredible that a loaded animal can pass. In the dry season the stream is fordable, the water reaching only to the saddle girths; but in the rainy season it is often impassable. The water is remarkably clear and pure, and I observed one or two small fishes in the pools.

The Maure is a tributary of the Desaguadero, the outlet of Lake Titicaca, and falls into that stream about midway in its course between the lake just named and that of Aullagas. Its left bank is less precipitous than the right, though abrupt, and we toiled slowly up its acclivity to the broken plain, in which the bed of the river is only a fissure or rent, invisible at the distance of a few hundred yards. At three o'clock the ground became more broken and we became involved among a series of hills, our path ascending and descending, and crossing at intervals narrow, swampy valleys, where patches of green and tremulous sod alternated with dark, deep pools of water, affording a scant pasturage for some droves of alpacas, which find a congenial home in these localities. At various points we observed rough stone inclosures in which the alpacas are herded for clipping and other purposes, and which, perhaps, date beyond the conquest. But nowhere could we discern a trace of human habitation. In some sheltered spots we noticed a few dwarf quinua, or wild olive trees, with trunks rarely over an inch in diameter, and which are carefully protected by the arrieros, to whom they afford a desirable substitute as fuel for the dung of the vicuña and llama. The latter, as I have said, is about the only kind of fuel to be had in the Altos of Peru; and even this would be scant and difficult to get if it were not the unvarying habit of all the members of the llama family to make their droppings in certain fixed spots, where they form accumulations or mounds often ten to twelve feet broad, and from two to five feet high. These black heaps are characteristic features in the puny landscapes.

Toward night we began to climb the high ridge known as the Pass of Chuluncayani. The summit of the ridge, according to Pentland, is 15,160 feet above the sea, and from it we caught our first view, over lofty and rugged intervening ridges, of the Nevados of the Andes— that magnificent snowy range that dwarfs the Alps, and stretches in a glittering line along the horizon for three hundred miles. The descent of the ridge was almost as difficult and dangerous as that into the gorge of the Rio Maure, but much longer and wearisome. Both H— and myself broke the cruppers of our saddles under the sudden plunges of the mules, and in many places, in common with our arrieros, we were obliged to dismount and proceed on foot. At the base of the ridge we came to a small, wet pampa, or plain, sloping somewhat rapidly to the right and traversed by half a dozen bright and brawling rivulets, falling from a high ridge on the north. On the further edge of the plain, which, from its abundance of water and favorable exposure to the sun, was relatively fresh and green, we saw the buildings of the tambo of Chuluncayani—a welcome sight through the cold mist that had already begun to rise from the damp surface of the pampa.

The keeper of the tambo, which is much larger and better appointed than that of Tacora, is by far the most enterprising and active man that I met with in Bolivia. He had several flocks of alpacas scattered in the surrounding valleys, kept a store of barley straw for the mules of travelers, and was able to furnish the traveler himself with a chicken, if he chose to pay therefor the sum of three dollars. His chupe was less thin than we found to be the average quality of that kind of delicacy; and, in bottles bearing labels gorgeous in crimson and gold, he had brandy of the kind that Berrios called may endemoniado, and in which red pepper seemed to be the predominant ingredient. And, although the floor of the room set apart for travelers was the bare earth, innocent of brush or broom, yet were not its walls gay with paper only less dazzling than the labels of his brandy bottles? We had a chupe and two chickens, returned one of the two bottles of brandy, and had barley straw for our mules, for which our enterprising host charged me sixty-four dollars! There was no charge for bedding and lights, for these we supplied ourselves. From this statement the adventurer in Southern Peru and Bolivia may form some estimate of the expense of travel in those interesting regions. Sixteen cents a pound, or at the rate of $320 a ton, is the current charge in Chuluncayani for green barley straw — "market firm." I left my Bolivian friends disputing with the landlord because he had charged them four dollars each.

Beyond Chuluncayani the road winds through a hilly country, constantly descending, until, in a beautiful little savanna, or pampa, completely hemmed in by hills, it crosses the Rio Santiago, a stream flowing nearly due east, between parallel ranges of hills artificially terraced, and where we saw the first signs of cultivation we had discovered since leaving Palca. These andenes, or terraces, became familiar enough before we left the Sierra, but here they were welcome indications of the proximity of human beings. The crops were all gathered, but we learned that barley, quinua, and potatoes, were cultivated on these sunny hillsides. Barley does not ripen, and is cultivated only for fodder. Following down the Rio Santiago, we finally came to some isolated buildings, in one of which was a cretin afflicted with concomitant goitre, who, except in color, might be mistaken for one of the miserable wretches so common in Switzerland and the Tyrol.

The valley now began to widen, and soon spread out into a broad plain, on a slight eminence in which we discerned the village of Santiago de Machaca. The stream or river here deflects to the left, and not to the right, as laid down in the maps, and pursues a northeastern course. Numberless water fowls, including geese, ducks of various kinds, several varieties of water hens and ibises, disported themselves in its icy waters, or flew away, screaming, on our approach.

At noon we reached the village, which has a population of between five and six hundred souls, chiefly occupied in raising llamas, for which the broad plain is favorable. The plaza in the centre of the town is large, and the streets entering it at each corner are covered with arches and flanked by little open chapels of adobes, in each of which is a mud altar surmounted by a wooden cross covered with tinsel and weighed down with withered mountain flowers. A low, rambling church, with a dilapidated bell tower standing apart, occupies one side of the plaza, facing the cabildo, with a prison on one hand confining two or three dirty and emaciated wretches, and a schoolroom on the other, in which a dozen children were learning a prayer, viva voce, but in which they stopped short as we rode past, and seemed to relish the opportunity to exclaim, "Buenos dias caballeros!" We had been recommended to the cura, who was rather noted in the Sierra for his intelligence and hospitality, but found that he had died a few weeks previously, and that his house was shut up. There was, however, a kind of pulperia, or shop, fronting on the plaza, where bayeta, or baize, was sold, and some rough woolen cloth of native manufacture, besides cheese, charqui (sun-dried beef), and eggs. We purchased the entire stock of the latter, and took our dinner on the sunny side of the building.

In Santiago the houses are built of adobes or compacted mud, and all are thatched with ichu grass. They seldom consist of more than a single apartment, entered by a low and narrow door, closed by a dried hide inside, the sill of which is raised so as to prevent the water from flowing in from the street. The walls of all of them incline inward, after the style characteristic of all the Inca edifices that we afterward had occasion to examine; and the doors were also narrower at the top than at the bottom, precisely as in the ancient structures. There are no "party walls" or single walls answering for contiguous houses, but each building has its distinct gables.

It was in Santiago that we saw for the first time the extraordinary montero, or hat, universally worn by the women of the Aymara race or family. It may be compared, not inaptly, to a coffin, with a kind of black valance suspended around a stiff body of pasteboard, covered with red cloth and tinsel. Nearly all the Indian women had children, silent, uncomplaining little creatures, slung in a thick shawl over their shoulders.

Style of Houses in Santiago de Machaca

Striking across the plain of Santiago, which extends to the northeast almost to the outlet of Lake Titicaca, where it is relieved by a number of mammiform hills or buttes, and which is dotted all over with heaps of llama dung, and sprinkled with the llamas themselves, we came to a little isolated church, with no building near, and with scarcely a hut in sight. I suppose some sort of pilgrimage or procession to it takes place on occasion, but as the church of Santiago was disproportionally large for the town, this edifice seemed entirely supererogatory. Just beyond it, in a little hollow, was the dead body of a mule, from which a group of condors were tearing the flesh in great strips, while a dozen or more of king vultures, gorgeous in color, were ranged in a circle around, respectfully waiting until their masters were gorged, when it would be their turn to take part in the unsavory feast. I fired at the group from the back of my mule, but owing to the wonderful trajectory of my rifle, with whose vagaries I had not yet become familiar, I missed my aim. After a series of ungraceful leaps, flapping their wings the while, for a hundred yards along the ground, the great birds succeeded in rising in the air, and commenced to circle in defiant and threatening evolutions above our heads. I dismounted for surer work, and with my second shot brought down one of the largest with a broken wing. But like the wounded vicuña on the stony plain of Tacora, he was more than a match, on his legs, for our worn and battered mules, and after a chase of half a mile I gave up pursuit, consoling myself with the reflection, what could I have done with the gigantic scavenger had I caught him?

Aaymara Female Headdress

Our halting place for the night was fixed at the village of San Andres de Machaca, and we pushed forward over some low ranges of hills with all our energy to reach it before dark. We passed some terraced slopes, subdivided by stonewalls, resembling fortifications, which were the huertas or gardens of St. Andres; crossed some streams flowing northward in shifting channels through an alluvial valley, and at five o'clock reached the irregular and rambling village for which we were bound. Our Bolivians, whose feet were literally "on their native heath," had taken great airs on themselves at Santiago, but they now became imperious. They rode to the house of the gobernador as if he were a born vassal; but that official had discovered our approach and hidden himself, a common expedient with alcaldes not addicted to hospitality, or else he was really absent from home. At any rate his poor habitation was shut up and tenantless. Our next recourse was to the cura, who lived in a relatively grand house behind the church, but he too was absent. His supliente or substitute, a pleasant young man, was in charge of the establishment, and gracefully accepted the situation, giving us a vacant room, and treating us to chupe and eggs.

The church of San Andres was the first one we had seen of that series of fine temples reared by the Jesuits in their days of prosperity and power in all parts of the Titicaca basin. Almost every squalid village has its church—always of good architectural design, and often of grand proportions and wonderful solidity. That of San Andres had never been finished, but was nevertheless imposing. Its facade is relieved by a lofty archway with a bold sweep, and its towers rise with a strength showing that the designer of the building was no feeble or timid architect. In front is an elaborate cross of beautiful white berenguela or alabaster, taken from extensive quarries of that material not far distant. Slabs or plates of this supply the place of glass in the windows of many of the churches of the Sierra, and give to the transmitted light a soft and mellow tinge like that let through the painted windows of old cathedrals.

We left San Andres before daylight, and resumed our course toward Nasacara, or, as the point is sometimes called, the Balsas of Nasacara, on the Rio Desaguadero. The morning was bitterly cold, and we suffered much until the sun rose and thawed the icicles from our beards. The country retains its aspect of a high plain, without cultivation, and covered with tola. At nine o'clock, having traveled five leagues, we came to the edge of the tableland, and obtained our first view of the valley of the Desaguadero, covered with sward, broken here and there by small patches of cultivated ground, and traversed up, and down, as far as the eye can reach, by the broad and placid river. At our feet, built partly on the hither, but mainly on the farther bank of the stream, is the village of Nasacara, distinguished chiefly for its bridge of balsas or floats of totora or reeds, and as being the point where the Bolivian customhouse is established, where passports are scrutinized and baggage fumbled.

The bridge of Nasacara is a type of a considerable number of bridges in South America, and merits more than a passing notice. It is a floating bridge, not unlike that across the Rhine at Cologne, except that, owing to the entire absence of timber in the country, the floats are of dried reeds, bound together in huge bundles, or balsas, pointed at the ends like canoes. These are fastened together by great cables of braided reeds, anchored to firm stone towers on both banks. The roadway is also of reeds resting on the floats, about four feet wide, and raised above the floats about the same height—a rather yielding and unsteady path, over which only one or two mules are allowed to pass at a time. The causeways leading to both extremities of the bridge are barred by gates at which toll is collected. When the river is swollen and the current very strong, it is usual to cut the cables at one extremity or the other, and let the bridge swing down the stream so as to prevent it being swept away.

Balsa Bridge Over The Rio Desacuardero

At the point where the bridge crosses the Desaguadero the river is 150 feet wide and 30 feet deep, flowing with a strong but even current. This point is about 40 miles below where the river debouches from Lake Titicaca, and 130 feet, according to Mr. Pentland's observations, below the level of the lake; thus giving to the river a fall to Nasacara of 31 feet to the mile. I nowhere saw rapids in the stream, nor did I hear of falls, and was told that it was easy to ascend the river in canoes to the lake itself. However that may be, nothing can be more absurd than the story which once found place in some educational publications that the waters of Lake Titicaca sometimes flow into Lake Aullagas, and vice versa, varying with the amount of rainfall, etc., in the northern and southern parts of this great terrestrial basin. Mr. Pentland fixes the level of Lake Aullagas at 570 feet lower than that of Lake Titicaca, and the distance between the two at about 170 miles, which would give an average fall throughout corresponding with that between Lake Titicaca and Nasacara. I have no doubt the river throughout is practicable for small boats, and that no serious interruption by rapids exists at any point.

We experienced no detention from the custom officers of Nasacara, although they exhibited unnecessary curiosity regarding my breech loading rifle, which I really believe they would have confiscated if they could have satisfied themselves how to use it, and how to replace the fixed ammunition without which it would have been useless. They gave us chupe and sold us cheese, and a little puno butter which comes packed in small bladders like snuff.

Here our Bolivians separated from us to pursue their road to La Paz, and Berrios coolly proposed to do the same thing, and leave us in charge of a dark and sinister looking arriero whom he had met, and who was in some way a dependent of his, but who had never been over the road we were to follow, and could not speak a word of Aymara or Quichua, now the universal languages of the country. My remonstrances were equally forcible and effective, and as they were made in the open street, must have been edifying to the good people of Nasacara. At noon we struck off from the town at right angles to the La Paz road, following up the valley of the river, over an undulating but uninhabited plain, to Jesus de Machaca, situated in marshy ground, near the base of the high ridge that separates the valley of the Desaguadero from that of Tiahuanaco. Its inhabitants are all Indians of the Aymara family, who eke out a scanty subsistence as shepherds and cultivators of the bitter variety of potato to which I have alluded, and which grows on the sunny hillsides. Like San Andres it has a great church in good repair, and containing some large pictures the excellence of which we were unable to judge under the "dim religious light" that stole through the alabaster windows. Having no place of refuge we rode direct to the house of the cura, who was neither a drunkard nor an adulterer, and in both these respects an exception to the wretches who in general profane the sanctuaries of God in Bolivia and Southern and Central Peru. He was an intelligent, meek, earnest man, who did for us all that we were unable to do for ourselves, and made no apologies for deficiencies which were obviously inseparable from his position. We passed the evening pleasantly in his society. He showed us through his church, in which five times the population of his village might easily assemble, and pointed out the beauties of its architecture with a faint flush of pride. His hectic cheek and rasping cough told us then that he verged on the close of his earthly career; and we were not surprised, although we were grieved, to hear a few months later, and before we left the Sierra, that the good cura of Jesus de Machaca, Manuel Valdivia, was dead.

The ridge behind Jesus de Machaca reaches close up to Lake Titicaca, and extends southward for a hundred miles, nearly parallel with the Desaguadero. The path over it is little frequented, rough, and in some places dangerous. We were from six o'clock in the morning until noon in reaching its summit, marked by the inevitable apacheta or cairn of stones, standing at an elevation of 3600 feet above the valley of the Desaguadero, and 16,500 feet above the sea.

It was from this point that we obtained our first view of Lake Titicaca, or rather of the lower and lesser lake of Tiqnina, with its high islands and promontories, and shores belted with reeds. It was here, too, that the great snowy chain of the Andes, of which we had only caught glimpses before, burst on our sight in all its majesty. Dominating the Lake is the massive bulk of Illampu, or Sorata, the crown of the continent, the highest mountain of America, rivaling, if not equaling in height, the monarchs of the Himalaya. Observers vary in their estimates and calculations of its altitude from 25,000 to 27,000 feet; my own estimates place it at not far from 26,000. Extending southward from this is an uninterrupted chain of nevados, or snowy mountains, nowhere less than 20,000 feet in height, which terminates in the great mountain of Illamini, 24,500 feet in altitude. Between the eminence on which we stand and these gigantic mountains is, first, the deep valley and plain of Tiahuanaco, with a high tableland or puno succeeding, and a range of mountains beyond, which look small only from contrast with their snow crowned neighbors.

Looking back, the view, if not equally imposing, is nevertheless as interesting. We can trace the windings of the Desaguadero through its shallow valley until lost in the distance in the direction of Lake Aullagas. There, too, is the broad plain of Santiago over which we have toiled, its inequalities scarcely discernible from our elevation. Beyond it, distinct, white, grand, and solemn, the volcanic peaks of Sahama, Pomarape, and Tacora, the pinnacles of the Cordilleras, and themselves reflecting their silver crests in the Pacific.

Nowhere else in the world, perhaps, can a panorama so diversified and grand be obtained from a single point of view. The whole great tableland of Peru and Bolivia, at its widest part, with its own system of waters, its own rivers and lakes, its own plains and mountains, all framed in by the ranges of the Cordillera and the Andes, is presented like a map before the adventurous visitor who climbs to the apacheta of Tiahuanaco. Grand, severe, almost sullen is the aspect which nature presents here. We stand in the centre of a scenery and a terrestrial system which seems to be in spirit, as well as in fact, lifted above the rest of the world, coldly and calmly looking down upon it, sharing none of its sympathies, and disturbed by none of its alarms. The silent, wondering vicuña, the gliding llama, the great condor circling high up in the air, or sailing down toward us as if in menace, the absence of forests, the clouds surging up from the dank plains and forests of Brazil, only to be precipitated and dissolved by the snowy barriers which they can not pass, the clear metallic blue sky above, the keen sunlight, the awful silence— all impress the traveler with the feeling that he is no longer in the world that he has known before. There is nothing with which he is familiar, nothing in the way of association or suggestive of other scenes. Not an unfitting region this for the development of an original civilization like that which has carved its memorials in massive stones, and left them in the plain of Tiahuanaco at our feet, and of which no tradition remains except that they were the work of giants, who reared them in a single night.

The descent into the valley or plain of Tiahuanaco is more abrupt than in the direction of the Desaguadero, and the most reckless travelers find it requisite to dismount and proceed on foot. It was dark when we struck the edge of the plain, and ascertained that we had yet nearly four leagues to go before reaching the village of Tiahuanaco. This border of the plain receives the wash of the adjacent ridge, and is covered thickly with rocky debris, and seamed with shallow torrent beds. To get at the soil and protect the ground when once reclaimed, the stones in many places have been heaped together in mounds, or long, heavy ridges, capable of resisting or diverting the rush of the waters descending from the hills. This work seems to have been in great part, if not wholly, performed by the ancient inhabitants; showing that here, as everywhere else, they were avaricious of arable soil, and spared neither time nor labor to rescue the scantiest portion of it to cultivation.

View of Lake Titicaca and Illampu, The Crown of the Andes

At a distance of two leagues from the western border of the plain we came to a considerable swell of land, free from stones, and of which considerable patches were broken up for crops; and a league and a half further, after fording a shallow stream of clear running water, we reached the village of Tiahuanaco itself, situated upon another slight elevation, in a well chosen position. The narrow, unlighted streets, lined by low huts of rough stones laid in clay, covered with thatch, destitute of windows, and entered only by low and narrow doorways, closed for the most part with raw hides, were silent and deserted; the wretched inhabitants have hardly fuel wherewith to cook their scanty food, and are fain to slink away into their dark and squalid habitations as soon as the sun withdraws his genial rays. The traveler who emerges in the morning, blue and benumbed from his bed on the ground in an unventilated, gloomy hut of the Sierra, where the pigs are not his most unpleasant companions, to thaw himself into life on the sunny side of the wretched chosa that has sheltered him, will readily comprehend how the people of Peru became worshipers of the sun.

We were not long in finding the plaza of Tiahuanaco, where a faint light shining out from a single portada in front of the church gave us the first evidence that the town possessed inhabitants. The house proved to be the posta, and the most we could learn from the saturnine Indians in charge was that the master of the post was absent. They neither invited us to come in, nor made any movement to assist us when we dismounted, but disappeared one by one into dark dormitories, leaving us standing alone, hungry and cold, in the open court. However, the arrival of our arrieros, some of whom spoke Aymara, changed the aspect of affairs. They pushed open the door of the principal or travelers apartment, and, piling the barley in stalk which it contained at one end, cleared a space for the single piece of furniture in the room—a broken table—and with imperative words and acts as emphatic, finally secured for us a dish of diluted chupe.

While this was going on we received a visit from the cura, on his return probably from some nocturnal adventure. His face was red and bloated, deeply scarred by smallpox, but retaining traces of original manly beauty. He was quite drunk and not very coherent, and when we began to question him about the celebrated ancient ruins of the neighborhood he became suddenly silent, and drew me into a dark corner of the courtyard, where, in a mysterious whisper, he told me that he knew all about the tapadas, or hidden treasures, and that we could count on his guidance in obtaining them, for an equitable division of the spoils. It was in vain I protested that we were not money diggers; he could not conceive how any stranger should evince an interest in the "vestiges of the Gentiles" not founded on the hope of discovering treasure among them. And here I may mention that throughout all of our explorations, in all parts of Peru, whether in the city or in the field, we were supposed to be searching for tapadas, and were constantly watched and followed by people who hoped to get some clew to the whereabouts of the treasures through our indications. Often, when engaged in surveys of fortifications or buildings, we found the marks left by us at night, to guide us in resuming our work in the morning, not only removed, but the earth deeply excavated below them. The ancient monuments of the country have suffered vastly more from the hands of treasure seekers than from fanatic violence, time, and the elements combined. The work of destruction from this cause has been going on for three hundred years, and still actively continues.

TIAHUANACO—THE BAALBEC OF THE NEW WORLD.

Indians Celebrating the Chuno or Potato Festival, Tiahuanaco

TIAHUANACO lies almost in the centre of the great terrestrial basin of Lakes Titicaca and Aullagas, and in the heart of a region which I have already characterized as the Thibet of the New World. This basin is perhaps the most interesting of the class of physical phenomena to which it belongs, and of which we have two other notable examples on this continent, viz.; the great Utah or Salt Lake basin within our own territories, and that of Lake Itza or Peten in Central America. They may all be described as portions of the continent, of greater or less elevation, entirely surrounded by mountains, or else as broad depressions in the earth's surface, with fluvial systems and water reservoirs of their own, and with no outlets to the sea.

The limits of the Titicaca basin on the south are not yet accurately determined; but calculating from the Pass of La Raya on the north, in latitude 14° 50' S., it may be estimated to have a length of between 600 and 700 miles, while its width, calculated by the reach of the streams that concentrate in it, may be taken to average not far from 200 miles; thus giving it a total area of about 120,000 square miles, or three times that of the State of New York. As we have seen, this basin is bounded on the west by the great chain of the Cordillera, the true back bone of the continent, and on the east by the Bolivian Andes, the loftiest section of that mighty range. Its slope is gentle toward the south. In its northern and highest portion reposes Lake Titicaca, a magnificent body of fresh water, comparable only with our North American lakes in respect of size, and lying at the extraordinary elevation of 12,864 feet above the sea. It receives several large, and at some seasons unfordable, streams, and, as we have seen, discharges its waters through a broad, deep, and rapid but not turbulent stream, El Desaguadero, which receives several considerable tributaries in its course, and pours a heavy flood of water into Lake Aullagas. Of the size, contour, and depth of the latter we know next to nothing, but it is positively asserted that it has no visible outlet to the sea. It has been suggested that it discharges itself into the Pacific through a subterranean channel, beneath the Cordillera, and that the Rio Loa, falling into the sea in latitude 21° 15' S., derives its waters from this source. On the other hand, it has been contended that the excess of water in the lake is carried off by evaporation, in which case its superficies must be vast indeed. In fact, Lake Aullagas is an unsolved geographical problem, and the most interesting one that the continent affords.

It is at Tiahuanaco, in the centre of this vast basin, at an elevation of 12,900 feet above the sea, in a broad, open, unprotected plain, arid in soil, cold in the wet and frigid in the dry season, that we find the evidences of an ancient civilization, regarded by many as the oldest and the most advanced of both American continents. It was to explore and investigate the monumental remains that have made this spot celebrated. I had come to Tiahuanaco, and I lost no time in commencing my task of exploration. This was not an easy one, for even with the aid of the drunken cura we were unable to procure laborers to assist us, for not only had we reached the village on the eve of the potato or chuño festival (a remnant of ancient observances), but before we had finished our work the Feast of Corpus had commenced; chicha flowed like water, and the few inhabitants that the chuño festival had left sober deliberately gave themselves up to beastly intoxication. The death of my photographer had left me with an elaborate and costly apparatus on my hands, with little knowledge of the theory and less of the practice of photography, and with the alternative of taking upon myself a work which I had not contemplated assuming, but which I had regarded as indispensable to the success of my undertaking. I had but a single assistant, Mr. Harvey, an amateur draftsman, of limited experience, and only such other aid as I could get from my muleteer and his men, who were eager to conclude their engagement, and simply astounded that we should waste an hour, much more that we should spend days, on the remains of the Gentiles. Still the investigation was undertaken, with equal energy and enthusiasm, and, I am confident, with as good results as could be reached without an expenditure of time and money which would hardly have been rewarded by any probable additional discoveries.

We spent a week in Tiahuanaco, going early to the ruins and returning late, and I believe obtained a plan of every structure that is traceable, and of every monument of importance that is extant.

The first thing that strikes the visitor in the village of Tiahuanaco is the great number of beautifully cut stones, built into the rudest edifices, and paving the squalidest courts. They are used as lintels, jambs, seats, tables, and as receptacles for water. The church is mainly built of them; the cross in front of it stands on a stone pedestal which shames the symbol it supports in excellence of workmanship. On all sides are vestiges of antiquity from the neighboring ruins, which have been a real quarry, whence have been taken the cut stones, not only for Tiahuanaco and all the villages and churches of its valley, but for erecting the cathedral of La Paz, the capital of Bolivia, situated in the deep valley of one of the streams falling into the River Beni, 20 leagues distant. And what is true here is also, I may add, true of most parts of the Sierra. The monuments of the past have furnished most of the materials for the public edifices, the bridges, and highways of the present day.

The ruins of Tiahuanaco have been regarded, by all students of American Antiquities, as in many respects the most interesting and important, and at the same time most enigmatical of any on the continent. Unique, yet perfect in type and harmonious in style, they appear to be the work of a people who were thorough masters of an architecture which had no infancy, passed through no period of growth, and of which we find no other examples. Tradition, which mumbles more or less intelligibly of the origin of many other American monuments, is dumb concerning these. The wondering Indians told the first Spaniards that "they existed before the sun shone in the heavens," that they were raised by giants, or that they were the remains of an impious people whom an angry Deity had converted into stone because they refused hospitality to his vice-gerent and messenger.

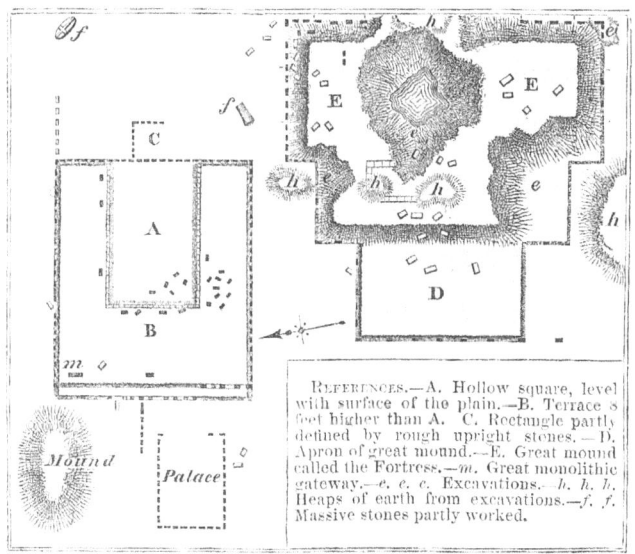

REFERENCES.—A. Hollow square, level with surface of the plain.—B. Terrace s feet higher than A. C. Rectangle partly defined by rough upright stones.—D. Apron of great mound.—E. Great mound called the Fortress.—m. Great monolithic gateway.—e. e. e. Excavations.—h. h. h. Heaps of earth from excavations.—f. f. Massive stones partly worked.

Plan of Part or the Ruins of Tiahuanaco

Reserving all speculations for another place, I shall give here only a rapid, but perhaps sufficiently minute, account of these remains, correcting some of the errors and avoiding some of the extravagances of my predecessors in the same field of inquiry. I must confess I did not find many things that they have described; but that fact, in view of the destructiveness of tapada hunters, and the rapacity of ignorant collectors of antiquities, does not necessarily discredit their statements. For Tiahuanaco is a rifled ruin, with comparatively few yet sufficient evidences of former greatness.

The ruins are about half a mile to the southward of the village, separated from it by a small brook and a shallow valley. The high road to La Paz passes close to them, in fact between them and some mounds of earth which were probably parts of the general system. They are on a broad and very level part of the plain, where the soil is an arenacious loam, firm and dry. Rows of erect stones, some of them rough or but rudely shaped by art; others accurately cut and fitted in walls of admirable workmanship; long sections of foundations, with piers and portions of stairways; blocks of stone, with mouldings, cornices, and niches cut with geometrical precision; vast masses of sandstone, trachyte, and basalt but partially hewn; and great monolithic doorways, bearing symbolical ornaments in relief, besides innumerable smaller, rectangular, and symmetrically shaped stones, rise on every hand, or lie scattered in confusion over the plain. It is only after the intelligent traveler has gone over the whole area and carefully studied the ground that the various fragments fall into something like their just relations, and the design of the whole becomes comprehensible.

Leaving aside, for the present, the lesser mounds of earth to which I have alluded, we find the central and most conspicuous portion of the ruins, which altogether cover not far from a square mile, to consist of a great, rectangular mound of earth, originally terraced, each terrace supported by a massive wall of cut stones, and the whole surmounted by structures of stone, parts of the foundations of which are still distinct. This structure is popularly called the "Fortress," and, tradition affirms, suggested the plan of the great fortress of Sacsahuaman, dominating the city of Cuzco. The sides of this structure, as also of all the others in Tiahuanaco, coincide within ten degrees with the cardinal points of the compass. Close to the left of the "Fortress"—and I adopt the name and the others I may use solely to facilitate description —is an area called the "Temple," slightly raised, defined by lines of erect stones, but ruder than those which surround the "Fortress." A row of massive pilasters stand somewhat in advance of the eastern front of this area, and still in advance of this are the deeply imbedded piers of a smaller edifice of squared stones, with traces of an exterior corridor, which has sometimes been called the "Palace." At other points, both to the south and northward, are other remains, to which later I shall have occasion to refer.

The structure called the "Temple" will claim our first attention; primarily because it seems to be the oldest of the group, the type, perhaps, of the others, and because it is here we find the great monolithic sculptured gateway of Tiahuanaco, which is absolutely unique, as far as our knowledge goes, on this continent.

The body of the "Temple' forms a rectangle of 388 by 445 feet, defined, as I said before, by lines of erect stones, partly shaped art. They are mostly of red sandstone, and of irregular size and height; those at the corners being more carefully squared and tallest. For the most part they are between 8 and 10 feet high, from 2 to 4 feet broad, and from 20 to 30 inches in thickness. The portions entering the ground, like those of our granite gate posts, are largest, and left so for the obvious purpose of giving the stones greater firmness in their position.

These stones, some of which have fallen and others disappeared, seem to have been placed, inclining slightly inward, at approximately 15 feet apart, measuring from centre to centre, and they appear to have had a wall of rough stones built up between them, supporting a terreplein of earth, about 8 feet above the general level of the plain. On its eastern side this terreplein had an apron or lower terrace 18 feet broad, along the edge of the central part of which were raised 10 great stone pilasters, placed 154 feet apart, all of which, perfectly aligned, are still standing with a single exception. They are of varying heights, and no two agree in width or thickness. The one that is fallen, which was second in the line, measures 13 feet 8 inches in length by 5 feet 8 inches in breadth. It is partly buried in the earth, but shows 32 inches of thickness above ground. Among those still erect the tallest is 14 feet by 4 feet 2 inches, and 2 feet 8 inches; the shortest 9 feet by 2 feet 9 inches, and 2 feet 5 inches. These are less in dimensions than the stones composing the inner cell or sanctum of Stonehenge, which range from 16 feet 3 inches to 21 feet 6 inches in height; but they are nearly if not quite equal with those composing the outer circle of that structure. They are much more accurately cut than those of Stonehenge, the fronts being perfectly true, and the backs alone left rough or only partially worked. The tops of the taller ones have shoulders cut into them as if to receive architraves, and as this feature does not appear in the shorter ones it may be inferred that their tops have been broken off, and that originally they were all of one length.

The American Stonehenge

And here I may call attention to another singular feature of this colonnade—namely, that the sides or edges of each erect stone are slightly cut away to within six inches of its face, so as to leave a projection of about an inch and a half, as if to retain in place any slab fitted between the stones and prevent it from falling outward. The same feature is found in the stones surrounding the great mound or "Fortress," where its purpose becomes obvious, as we shall Soon see.

Such is the general character of the exterior propylon, if I may so call it, of the structure called the "Temple." But within the line of stones surrounding it there are other features which claim our attention. I have said that the interior is a mound of earth raised about 8 feet above the general level. But in the centre and toward the western side is an area sunk to the general level, 280 feet long by

190 feet broad. It was originally defined on three sides by walls of rough stones which rose above the surface of the mound itself, but which are now in ruins. If this sunken area communicated in any way with the more elevated interior parts of the structure the means of communication by steps or otherwise have disappeared. Across the end of the area not shut in by the mound, the line of stones which surround the "Temple" is continued without interruption; but outside and connected with it is part of a small square of lesser stones also erect, standing in the open plain.

Regarding the eastern side of the "Temple," marked by the line of pilasters which I have described, as the front, we find here, at the distance of 57 feet, the traces of a rectangular structure, to which I have alluded as "the Palace," which was composed of blocks of trachyte admirably cut, 8 to 10 feet long, by 5 feet broad, with remains of what appears to have been a corridor 30 feet broad extending around it. The piers which supported "the Palace" still remain, sunk deep in the ground, and apparently resting on an even pavement of cut stones. Remove the superstructures of the best built edifices of our cities, and few if any would expose foundations laid with equal care, and none stones cut with such accuracy, or so admirably fitted together. And I may say, once for all, carefully weighing my words, that in no part of the world have I seen stones cut with such mathematical precision and admirable skill as in Peru, and no part of Peru are there any to surpass those which are scattered over the Plain of Tiahuanaco.

The so-called Palace does not seem to have been placed in any symmetrical relation toward the "Temple," although seemingly dependent on it; nor in fact do any of the ancient structures here appear to have been erected on any geometric plan respecting each other, such as is apparent in the arrangement of most of the remains of aboriginal public edifices in Peru.

The "Fortress" stands to the southwest of the "Temple," the sides of the two coinciding in their bearings, and is 64 feet distant from it. As I have already said, it is a great mound of earth, originally rectangular in shape, 620 feet in length, and 450 in width, and about 50 feet high. It is much disfigured by the operations of treasure seekers, who have dug into its sides and made great excavations from the summit, so that it resembles now rather a huge, natural, shapeless heap of earth than a work of human hands. The few of the many stones that environed it, and which the destroyers have spared, nevertheless enable us to make out its original shape and proportions. There are distinct evidences that the body of the mound was terraced, for there are still standing stones at different elevations, distant horizontally 18 and 30 feet from the base. There may have been more terraces than these lines of stones would indicate, but it is certain that there were at least three before reaching the summit. This coincides with what Garcilasso tells us of the mound when first visited by, the Spaniards. He says, speaking of the ruins under notice; "Among them there is a mountain or hill raised by hand, which, on this account, is most admirable. In order that the piled up earth should not be washed away and the hill leveled, it was supported by great walls of stone. No one knows for what purpose this edifice was raised." Cieza de Leon, who himself visited Tiahuanaco, soon after the conquest, gives substantially the same description of the so-called "Fortress."

Outer Terrace Walls of "Fortress" and Scattered Blocks of Stone

On the summit of this structure are sections of the foundations of rectangular buildings, partly undermined, and partly covered up by the earth from the great modern excavation in the centre, which is upward of 800 feet in diameter, and more than 60 feet deep. A pool of water stands at its bottom. This piece of barbarism, which, however, was only in continuation of some similar previous undertaking, was perpetrated within the last ten years by a man still living, formerly President of Bolivia, but whose name I shall not mention lest he should gain some portion of that notoriety which he values quite as highly as true reputation. All over the "Fortress" and on its slopes lie large and regular blocks of stone, sculptured with portions of elaborate designs, which would only appear when the blocks were fitted together.

Some portions of the outer or lower wall are fortunately intact, or nearly so, so that we are able to discover how it was constructed, and the plan and devices that were probably observed in all the other walls, as well as in some parts of the so-called "Temple." In the first place, large upright stones were planted in the ground, resting, there is reason to believe, on stone foundations. They are about ten feet above the surface, accurately faced, perfectly aligned, and inclining slightly inward toward the mound. They are placed 17 feet apart from centre to centre, and are very nearly uniform in size, generally about 3 feet broad and 2 feet in thickness. Their edges are cut to present the kind of shoulders to which I alluded in describing the pilasters in front of the "Temple," and of which the purpose now becomes apparent. The space between the upright stones is filled in with a wall of carefully worked stones. Those next the pilasters are cut with a shoulder to fit that of the pilaster they adjoin; and they are each, moreover, cut with alternate grooves and projections, like mortice and tenon, so as to fit immovably into each other horizontally. Vertically they are held in position by round holes drilled into the bottom and top of each stone at exact corresponding distances, in which, there is reason to believe; were placed short cylinders of bronze. We here see the intelligent devices of a people, unacquainted with the uses of cement, to give strength and permanence to their structures. Nearly all the blocks of stone scattered over the plain show the cuts made to receive what is called the T clamp, and the round holes to receive the metal pins that were to retain the blocks in their places, vertically.

The "Fortress" has on its eastern side an apron or dependent platform, 320 by 180 feet, of considerably less than half the elevation of the principal mound. Like the rest of the structure its outline was defined by upright stones, most of which, however, have disappeared.

The entrance to the "Fortress" seems to have been at its southeast corner, probably by steps, and to have been complicated by turnings from one terrace to another, something like those in some of the Inca fortresses.

The tradition runs that there are large vaults filled with treasure beneath the great mound, and that here commences a subterranean passage which leads to Cuzco, more than 400 miles distant. The excavations certainly reveal some curious subterranean features. The excavation at its southwest corner has exposed a series of superimposed cut stones, apparently resting on a pavement of similar character, 12 feet below the surface. It is said that Von Tschudi, when he visited the ruins, found some "caverns" beneath them (but whether under the "Fortress" or not does not appear), into which he endeavored to penetrate, but "was glad to be pulled out, as he soon became suffocated." I found no such subterranean vaults or passages in any part of Tiahuanaco; but I do not deny their existence.

To the southeast of the "Fortress," and about 250 paces distant, is a long line of wall in ruins, apparently a single wall, not connected with any other so as to form an inclosure. But beyond it are the remains of edifices of which it is now impossible to form more than approximate plans. One was measurably perfect thirty-three years ago, when visited by D'Orbigny, who fortunately has left a plan of it, more carefully made than of any of the others he has given us of ruins here or elsewhere. Since 1833, however, the iconoclasts have been at work with new vigor. Unable to remove the massive stones composing the base of what was called "The Hall of Justice," they mined them and blew them up with gunpowder, removing many of the elaborately cut fragments to pave the cathedral of La Paz. Enough remains to prove the accuracy of D'Orbigny's plan, and to verify what old Cieza de Leon wrote concerning these particular remains three hundred years ago.

The structure called "The Hall of Justice" occupied one end of a court something like that discoverable in "The Temple." In the first place we must imagine a rectangle, 420 feet long by 370 broad, defined by a wall of cut stones, supporting on three sides an interior platform of earth 130 feet broad, itself inclosing a sunken area, or court, also defined by a wall of cut stones. This court, which is of the general level of the plain, is 240 feet long and 160 broad. At its eastern end is, or rather was, the massive edifice distinguished as "The Hall of Justice," of which D'Orbigny says:

"It is a kind of platform of well cut blocks of stone, held together by copper clamps, of which only the traces remain. It presents a level surface elevated six feet above the ground, 131 feet long and 23 broad, formed of enormous stones, eight making the length and two the breadth. Some of these stones are twenty-five and a half feet long by fourteen feet broad, and six feet six inches thick. These are probably the ones measured by Cieza de Leon, who describes them as thirty feet long, fifteen in width, and six in thickness. Some are rectangular in shape, others of irregular form.

Lesser Monolithic Doorway

"On the eastern side of the platform, and cut in the stones of which they form part, are three groups of alcoves, or seats. One group occupies the central part of the monument, covering an extent of fifty-three feet, and is divided into seven compartments. A group of three compartments occupies each extremity of the monument. Between the central and side groups were reared monolithic doorways, similar in some respects to the large one described further on, only more simple, the one to the west alone having a sculptured frieze similar to that of the great gateway. [One of these, not however standing in its original position, is shown in the accompanying engraving.]

"In front of this structure, to the west, and about twenty feet distant, is a wall remarkable for the fine cutting of its stones, which are of a blackish basalt and very hard. The stones are all of equal dimensions, having a groove running around them, and each has a niche cut in it with absolute precision. Everything goes to show that the variety of the forms of the niches was one of the great ornaments of the walls, for on all sides we find stones variously cut, and evidently intended to fit together so as to form architectural ornaments."

So much for the description of D'Orbigny. I measured one of the blocks with a double niche, which is shown in the engravings of the terrace walls of the "Fortress." It is six feet two inches in length, three feet seven inches broad, and two feet six inches thick. The niches are sunk to the depth of three inches.

One of the monolithic doorways originally belonging to this structure is unquestionably that forming the entrance to the cemetery of Tiahuanaco. This cemetery is an ancient rectangular mound, about a hundred paces long, sixty broad, and twenty feet high, situated midway between the village and "the Fortress." Its summit is inclosed by an adobe wall, and, as I have said, the entrance is through an ancient monolithic gateway, of which I give a front and back view. It is seven feet five inches in extreme height, five feet ten and a half inches in extreme width, and sixteen and a half inches thick. The doorway, or opening, is six feet two inches in height, and two feet ten inches wide. The frieze has a repetition of the ornaments composing the lower line of sculptures of the great monolith, but it has suffered much from time and violence. The ornamentation of the back differs from that of the front, and seems to have been made to conform to the style adopted in the interior of the structure.

Gateway at Cemetary - Front View

In making our measurement in the cemetery we disturbed a pack of lean, hungry, savage dogs of the Sierra—an indigenous species—which had dug up the body of a newly buried child from its shallow, frozen grave, and were ravenously devouring it. They snarled at us with bristling backs and bloodshot eyes as we endeavored to drive them away from their horrible feast—by no means the first, as the numerous rough holes they had dug, the torn wrappings of the dead, and the skulls and fragments of human bodies scattered around too plainly attested. I subsequently represented the matter to the cura, but he only shrugged his shoulders, ejaculating; "What does it matter? They have been baptized, and all Indians are brutes at the best."

Returning to the so-called "Hall of Justice," we find, to the eastward of it, a raised area 175 feet square, and from 8 to 10 feet high, the outlines defined by walls of cut stone. This seems to have escaped the notice of travelers; at least it is not mentioned by them. In the centre of this area there seems to have been a building about 50 feet square, constructed of very large blocks of stone, which I have denominated "The Sanctuary." Within this, where it was evidently supported on piers, is the distinctive and most remarkable feature of the structure. It is a great slab of stone 13 feet 4 inches square, and 20 inches in thickness. It is impossible to describe it intelligibly, and I must refer to the engraving for a notion of its character.

Gateway at Cemetary - Rear View

It will be observed that there is an oblong area out in the upper face of the stone, 7 feet 3 inches long, 5 feet broad, and 6 inches deep. A sort of sunken "portico" 20 inches wide, 3 feet 9 inches long, is cut at one side, out of which opens what may be called the entrance, 22 inches wide, extending to the edge of the stone.

At each end of the "portico" is a flight of three miniature steps leading up to the general surface of the stone, and sunk in it, while at the side of the excavated area are three other flights of similar steps, but in relief. They lead to the broadest part of the stone, where there are six mortices, 8 inches square, sunk in the stone 6 inches, and forming two sides of a square, of 3 feet 7 inches on each side, and apparently intended to receive an equal number of square columns. The external corners of the stone are sharp, but within 6 inches of the surface they are cut round on a radius of 1 foot.

I can not resist the impression that this stone was intended as a miniature representation or model of a sacred edifice, or of some kind of edifice reared by the builders of the monuments of Tiahuanaco. The entrance to the sunken area in the stone, the steps leading to the elevation surrounding it, and the *naos* opposite the entrance, defined perhaps by columns of bronze or stone set in the mortices and supporting some kind of roof, constituting the shrine within which stood the idol or symbol of worship—all these features would seem to indicate a symbolic design in this monument. The building in which it stood, on massive piers that still remain, was constructed of blocks of stone, some of them nearly 14 feet in length and of corresponding size and thickness, and was not so large as to prohibit the probability that it was covered in.

Symbolical Slab

Look at the plan of the so-called "Temple," and of the inclosure to the area, one side of which was occupied by the building called "The Hall of Justice," and we can not fail to observe features suggestive of the plan cut in the great stone that I have called symbolical.

Front View of the Great Monolithic Gateway

The most remarkable monument in Tiahuanaco, as already intimated, is the great monolithic gateway. Its position is indicated by the letter m in the plan. It now stands erect, and is described as being in that position by every traveler except D'Orbigny, who visited the ruins in 1833, and who says it had then fallen down. I give two views of this unique monument, both from original photographs, of some interest to me as the first it was ever my fortune to be called on to take. It will be seen that it has been broken, the natives say by lightning; the fracture extending from the upper right hand angle of the opening, so that the two parts lap by each other slightly, making the sides of the doorway incline toward each other; whereas they are, or were, perfectly vertical and parallel —a distinguishing feature in all of the doorways and sculptures of Tiahuanaco.

This monolith has attracted so much attention, and the drawings that have been given of it have been so exceedingly erroneous, that I have sought to reproduce its features with the greatest care, using the line, the pencil, the photograph, and the cartridge paper mould.

Sculpted Figure on Great Monolith

We must imagine first a block of stone, somewhat broken and defaced on its edges, but originally cut with precision, 13 feet 5 inches long, 7 feet 2 inches high above ground, and 18 inches thick. Through its centre is cut a doorway, 4 feet 6 inches high, and 2 feet 9 inches wide. Above this doorway, and as it now stands on its southeast side or front, are four lines of sculpture in low relief, like the Egyptian plain sculptures, and a central figure, immediately ever the doorway, sculptured in high relief. On the reverse we find the doorway surrounded by friezes or cornices, and above it on each side two small niches, below which, also on either side, is a single larger niche. The stone itself is a dark and exceedingly hard trachyte. It is faced with a precision that no skill can excel; its lines are perfectly drawn, and its right angles turned with an accuracy that the most careful geometer could not surpass. Barring some injuries and defacements and some slight damages by weather, I do not believe there exists a better piece of stone cutting, the material considered, on this or the other continent. The front, especially the part covered by sculpture, has a fine finish, as near a true polish as trachyte can be made to bear.

The lower line of sculpture is 7+ inches broad, and is unbroken; the three above it are 8 inches high, cut up in cartouches or squares of equal width, but interrupted in the centre, immediately over the doorway, by the figure in high relief, to which I have alluded. This figure, with its ornaments, covers a space of 32 by 21 inches. There are consequently three ranges or tiers of squares on each side of this figure, 8 in each range, or 48 in all.

The figures represented in these squares have human bodies, feet, and hands; each holds a sceptre; they are winged; but the upper and lower series have human heads wearing crowns, represented in profile, while the heads of the sixteen figures in the line between them have the heads of condors.

The central and principal figure is angularly but boldly cut, in a style palpably conventional. Its head is surrounded by a series of what may be called rays, each terminating in a circle, the head of the condor, or that of a tiger, all conventionally, but forcibly treated. In each hand he grasps two staves or sceptres of equal length with his body, the lower end of the right hand sceptre terminating in the head of the condor, and the upper in that of the tiger, while the lower end of the left hand sceptre terminates in the head of the tiger, and the upper is bifurcate, and has two heads of the condor. The staves or sceptres are not straight and stiff, but curved as if to represent serpents, and elaborately ornamented as if to represent the sinuous action of the serpent in motion. The radiations from the head, which I have called rays, for want of a better term, seem to have the same action. An ornamented girdle surrounds the waist of this principal figure, from which depends a double fringe. It stands upon a kind of base or series of figures approaching nearest in character to the architectural ornament called grecques, each extremity of which, however, terminates in the crowned heads of the tiger or the condor. The face has been somewhat mutilated, but shows some peculiar figures extending from the eyes diagonally across the cheeks, terminating also in the heads of the animals just named.

The winged human headed and condor headed figures in the three lines of squares are represented kneeling on one knee, with their faces turned to the great central figure, as if in adoration, and each one holds before him a staff or sceptre. The sceptres of the figures in the two upper rows are bifurcate, and correspond exactly with the sceptre in the left hand of the central figure, while the sceptres of the lower tier correspond with that represented in his right hand. The relief of all these figures is scarcely over two-tenths of an inch; their minor features are indicated by very delicate lines, slightly incised, which form subordinate figures, representing the heads of condors, tigers, and serpents. Most of us have seen pictures and portraits of men and animals, which under close attention resolve themselves into representatives of a hundred other things, but which are so artfully arranged as to produce a single broad effect. So with these winged figures. Every part, the limbs, the garb, all separate themselves into miniatures of the symbols that run all through the sculptures, on this singular monument.

The fourth or lower row of sculpture differs entirely from the rows above it. It consists of repetitions—seventeen in all —smaller and in low relief, of the head of the great central figure, surrounded by corresponding rays, terminating in like manner with the heads of animals. These are arranged alternately at the top and bottom of the line of sculpture, within the zig-zags or grecques, and every angle terminates in the head of a condor. It is impossible to describe this arrangement of figures and ornament, and I should require a drawing to make what I have said intelligible.

The three outer columns of winged figures, and the corresponding parts of the lower line of sculpture are only blocked out, and have none of the elaborate, incised ornamentation discoverable in the central parts of the monument. A very distinct line separates these unfinished sculptures from those portions that are finished, which is most marked in the lower tier. On each side of this line, standing on the rayed heads to which I have alluded, placed back to back, and looking in opposite directions, are two small but interesting figures of men, crowned with something like a plumed cap, and holding to their mouths what appear to be trumpets. Although only three inches high, these little figures are ornamented in like manner with the larger ones, with the heads of tigers, condors, etc.

These are the only sculptures on the face of the great monolith of Tiahuanaco. I shall not attempt to explain their significance. D'Orbigny finds in the winged figures with human heads, symbols or representations of conquered chiefs coming to pay their homage to the ruler who had his capital in Tiahuanaco, and who, as the founder of Sun worship and the head of religion as of the state, was invested with divine attributes as well as with the insignia of power. The figures with condors' heads, the same fanciful philosopher supposes, may represent the chiefs of tribes who had not yet fully accepted civilization, and were therefore represented without the human profile, as an indication of their unhappy and undeveloped state. By parity of interpretation we may take it that the eighteen unfinished figures were those of as many chieftains as the ruler of Tiahuanaco had it in his mind to reduce, and of which, happily, just two-thirds had claims to be regarded as civilized, and, when absorbed, to be perpetuated with human heads and not with those of condors.

Another French writer, M. Angrand, finds a coincidence between these sculptures and those of Central America and Mexico, having a corresponding mythological and symbolical significance, thus establishing identity of origin and intimate relationship between the builders of Tiahuanaco and those of Palenque, Ocosingo, and Xochicalco.

Leibnitz tells us that nothing exists without a cause; and it is not to be supposed that the sculptures under notice were made without a motive. They are probably symbolical, but with no knowledge of the religious ideas and conceptions of the ancient people whose remains they are, it is presumptuous to attempt to interpret them. Nowhere else in Peru, or within the whole extent of the Inca empire, do we find any similar sculptures; and they are, as regards Inca art, quite as unique in Peru as they would be in Boston Common or the Central Park.,

The reverse of the great monolith shows a series of friezes over the doorway, five in number, of which the engraving will give a better idea than any description. Above the entrance on either hand are two niches, 12 by 9 inches in the excavation. It will be observed that those on the right have a sort of sculptured cornice above them which those on the left have not. The second one on the left, it will also be observed, is not complete, but evidently intended to be finished out on another block, which was to form a continuation of the wall of which the gateway itself was designed to be a part. Indeed, as I have said, nearly all the blocks of stone scattered over the plain are cut with parts of niches and other architectural features, showing that they were mere fragments of a general design, which could only be clearly apparent when they were properly fitted together.

Back of Great Monolith

The lower niches, now on a level with the ground, show that the monolith is sunk deeply in the soil. They exhibit some peculiar features. At each inner corner above and below are vertical sockets, apparently to receive the pivots of a door, extending upward and downward seven inches in the stone. D'Orbigny avers that he discovered the stains of bronze in these orifices; and I have no doubt that these niches had doors possibly of bronze hinged in these sockets, and so firmly that it was necessary to use chisels, the marks of which are plain, to cut into the stone and disengage them. These large niches are 28.2 inches by 18.2 inches wide.

I should mention that on the face of the monolith, on each side of the doorway, but near the edges of the stone, are two mortices 10 inches by 9 and 6 inches deep, and 12 inches by 6 and 4 inches deep respectively, which are not shown in the drawings published by D'Orbigny and some others.

I very much question if this remarkable stone occupies its original position. How far it has sunk in the ground it was impossible for me to determine, for the earth was frozen hard, and we had no means of digging down to ascertain. D'Orbigny, as I have already said, states it was fallen when he visited it. Who has since raised it, and for what purpose, it is impossible to say. No one that we could find either knew or cared to know anything about it. It seems to me not unlikely that it had a position in the hollow square of the structure called "The Temple," in some building corresponding with that called "The Hall of Justice." Or, perhaps, it had a place in the structure inclosing the stone I have ventured to call symbolical. It is neither so large nor so heavy that it may not be moved by fifty men with ropes, levers, and rollers; and although we do not now know of any reason why it should have been removed from its original position, we know that many of the heaviest stones have been thus moved, including the monolithic doorway at the entrance of the "Panteon" or cemetery.

In addition to the various features of Tiahuanaco already enumerated, I must not neglect to notice the vast blocks of unhewn and partially hewn stones, that evidently have never entered into any structure, which lie scattered among the ruins. The positions of two or three are indicated in the plan. The one to the northeast of "The Temple" is 26 x 17, and 3 ½ feet above ground. It is of red standstone, with deep grooves crossing each other at right angles in the centre, 20 inches deep, as if an attempt had been made to cut the stone into four equal parts. Another of nearly equal dimensions, partly hewn, lies between "The Temple" and "The Fortress." Another, boat shaped and curiously grooved, lies to the northwest of the great mound. It measures upward of 40 feet in length, and bears the marks of transportation from a considerable distance.

There were formerly a number of specimens of sculpture in Tiahuanaco, besides the two monolithic gateways I have described. Says Cieza de Leon; "Beyond this hill [referring to the Fortress] are two stone idols, of human shape, and so curiously carved that they seem to be the work of very able masters. They are as big as giants, with long garments differing from those the natives wear, and seem to have some ornament on their heads." These were broken in pieces, so D'Orbigny tells us, by blasts of powder inserted between the shoulders, and not even the fragments remain on the plain of Tiahuanaco. The head of one lies by the side of the road, four leagues distant, on the way to La Paz, whither an attempt was made to carry it. I did not see it, but I reproduce the sketch of it given by D'Orbigny, merely remarking that I have no doubt the details are quite as erroneous as those of the figures portrayed by the same author on the great monolith. The head is 3 feet 6 inches high, and 2 feet 7 inches in diameter; so that if the other proportions of the figure were corresponding, the total height of the statue would be about 18 feet. D'Orbigny found several other sculptured figures among the ruins; one with a human head and wings rudely represented; another of an animal resembling a tiger, etc. Castelnau mentions "an immense lizard cut in stone," and other sculptured figures. M. Angrand, whose notes have been very judiciously used by M. Desjardains, speaks of eight such figures in the village of Tiahuanaco, besides two in La Paz, and one, broken, on the road thither. I found but two; rough sculptures of the human head and bust, in coarse red sandstone, one of a man and the other of a woman, standing by the side of the gateway of the church of Tiahuanaco. They are between four and five feet high, roughly cut, much defaced, and more like the idols I found in Nicaragua, and have represented in my work on that country, than any others I have seen elsewhere.

I may mention here, that among the stones taken from the ruins and worked into buildings in the town of Tiahuanaco are a number of cylindrical columns cut from a single block, with capitals resembling the Doric. One of these stands on each side of the entrance to the court of the church, 6 feet high and 14 inches in diameter. There are also many caps of square columns or pilasters, besides numbers of stones cut with deep single or double grooves, as if to serve for water conduits when fitted together—a purpose the probability of which is sanctioned by finding some stones with channels leading off at right angles, like the elbows in our own water pipes.

Head of Statue at Tiahuanaco

The stones composing the structures of Tiahuanaco, as already said, are mainly red sandstone, slate colored trachyte, and a dark, hard basalt. None of these rocks are found *in situ* on the plain, but there has been much needless speculation as to whence they were obtained. There are great cliffs of red sandstone about five leagues to the north of the ruins, on the road to the Desaguadero; and, on the isthmus of Yunguyo, connecting the peninsula of Copacabana with the main land, are found both basaltic and trachytic rocks, identical with the stones in the ruins. Many blocks, hewn or partially hewn, are scattered over the isthmus. It is true this point is 40 miles distant from Tiahuanaco in a right line; and that, if obtained here, the stones mast have been carried 25 miles by water and 15 by land. That some of them were brought from this direction is indicated by scattered blocks all the way from the ruins to the lake; but it is difficult to conceive how they were transported from one shore to the other. There is no timber in the region whereof to construct rafts or boats, and the only contrivances for navigation are balsas or floats made of totora or reeds, closely bound into cylinders, tapering at the ends, which are turned up so as to give them something of the outline of boats. Before they become water soaked these floats are exceedingly light and buoyant.

Columns and Figures in Stone in Tiahuanaco

As to how the stones of Tiahuanaco were cut, and with what kind of instruments—these are questions which I do not now propose to discuss. I may nevertheless observe here that I have no reason to believe that the builders of Tiahuanaco had instruments differing essentially in form or material from those used by the Peruvians generally, which, it is certain, were of champi, a kind of bronze.

I have thus rapidly presented an outline of the remains of Tiahuanaco—remains most interesting, but in such an absolute condition of ruin as almost to defy inquiry or generalization. Regarding them as in some respects the most important of any in Peru, I have gone more into details concerning them than I shall do in describing the better preserved and more intelligible monuments with which we shall have, hereafter, to deal.

We find on a review that, apart from five considerable mounds of earth now shapeless with one exception, there are distinct and impressive traces of five structures, built of stones or defined by them, "The Fortress," "The Temple," "The Palace," "The Hall of Justice," and "The Sanctuary"—terms used more to distinguish than truly characterize them. The structure called "The Fortress" may indeed have been used for the purpose implied in the name. Terraced, and each terrace faced with stones, it may have been, as many of the terraced pyramids of Mexico were, equally temple and fortress, where the special protection of the divinity to whom it was reared was expected to be interposed against an enemy. But the absence of water and the circumscribed area of the structure seem to weigh against the supposition of a defensive origin or purpose. But whatever its object "The Fortress" dominated the plain, and when the edifices that crowned its summit were perfect it must have been by far the most imposing structure in Tiahuanaco. "The Temple" seems to me to be the most ancient of all the distinctive monuments of Tiahuanaco. It is the American Stonehenge. The stones defining it are rough and frayed by time. The walls between its rude pilasters were of uncut stones, and although it contains the most elaborate single monument among the ruins, and notwithstanding the erect stones constituting its portal are the most striking of their kind, it nevertheless has palpable signs of age, and an air of antiquity which we discover in none of its kindred monuments. Of course its broad area was never roofed in, whatever may have been the case with smaller, interior buildings no longer traceable. We must rank it, therefore, with those vast open temples—for of its sacred purpose we can scarcely have a doubt—of which Stonehenge and Avebury are examples, and which we find in Brittany, in Denmark, in Assyria, and on the Steppes of Tartary, as well as in our own Mississippi Valley. It seems to me to have been the nucleus around which the remaining monuments of Tiahuanaco sprung up, and the model upon which some of them were fashioned. How far, in shape or arrangement, it may have been symbolical I shall not undertake to say; but I think that students of antiquity are generally prepared to concede a symbolical significance to the primitive Pagan temples as well as to the cruciform edifices of Christian times.

We can hardly conceive of remains so extensive as those of Tiahuanaco, except as indices of a large population, and as evidences of the previous existence on or near the spot of a considerable city.

But we find nowhere in the vicinity any decided traces of ancient habitations; such as abound elsewhere in Peru, in connection with most public edifices. Again, the region around is cold, and for the most part arid and barren. Elevated 13,000 feet above the sea, no cereals grow except barley, which often fails to mature, and seldom if ever so perfects itself as to be available for seed. The maize is dwarf and scant, and uncertain in yield, and the bitter potato and quinua constitute almost the sole articles of food for the pinched and impoverished inhabitants. This is not, prima facie, a region for nurturing or sustaining a large population, and certainly not one wherein we should expect to find a capital. Tiahuanaco may have been a sacred spot or shrine, the position of which was determined by an incident, an augury, or a dream, but I can hardly believe that it was a seat of dominion.

Some vague traditions point to Tiahuanaco as the spot whence Manco Capac, the founder of the Inca dynasty, took his origin, and whence he started northward to teach the rude tribes of the Sierra religion and government; and some late writers, D'Orbigny and Castelnau among them, find reasons for believing that the whole Inca civilization originated here, or was only a reflex of that which found here a development, never afterward equaled, long before the golden staff of the first Inca sunk into the earth where Cuzco was founded, thus fixing through superhuman design the site of the imperial city.

But the weight of tradition points to the rocky islands of Lake Titicaca as the cradle of the Incas, whence Manco Capac and Mama Oella, his wife and sister, under the behest of their father, the Sun, started forth on their beneficent mission. Certain it is that this lake and its islands were esteemed sacred, and that on the latter were reared structures if not as imposing as many other and perhaps later ones, yet of peculiar sanctity.

But before starting on our visit to that lake and its islands, I must relate some of the incidents of our stay in Tiahuanaco.

I have no doubt the cura of the town believes to this day that our visit to the ruins was for the purpose of digging for treasures, and that we had some "itinerario," or guide, obtained from the archives of Old Spain to direct our search. What the Indians themselves thought they did not tell us. But on our very first day among the monuments, and within an hour after we had pitched our photographic tent and got out our instruments, we became aware of the presence of a very old man, withered, wrinkled, and bent with the weight of years. His hair was scant and gray, his eyes rheumy, and his face disfigured by a great quid of coca that he carried in one cheek. He wore a tattered pantaloons of coarse native cloth, made from the fleece of the llama, kept together by thongs; his poncho was old and ragged, and the long woolen cap that was pulled low over his forehead was greasy from use and stiff with dirt. He had an earthen vessel containing water suspended from his waist, besides a pouch of skin containing coca, and a little gourd of unslaked lime. In his hand he carried a small double edged stone cutter's pick or hammer. He paid us no perceptible attention, but wandered about deliberately among the blocks of cut stone that strew the ground, and finally selected one of a kind of white tufa, which he rolled slowly and with many a pause up to the very foot of the great monolith, then seated himself on the ground, placed it between his legs, and after preparing a new quid of coca, commenced to work on the stone, apparently with the purpose of cutting it in halves. He worked at it all day with scarcely perceptible effect, and during the whole time neither noticed us nor responded to our questions. Just before returning to the village, in the edge of the chill night, I prevailed on one of our arrieros, who could speak Aymara, to ask him what was his occupation. He got the curt answer from the old man that he was "cutting out a cross." Every morning he was at the ruins before us, and he never left until after we did at night. All day he pecked away at the stone between his knees, apparently absorbed in his work and oblivious of our presence. After a time we came to look upon him as an integral part of the monuments, and would have missed him as much as we would have done the great monolith itself.

One evening I mentioned the old man to the cura, who again put on mystery, took me out for a turn in the plaza, and explained in whispers, heavy with fumes of cañaso, that the old man was nothing more nor less than a spy on our doings, and that we made no movement in any direction that he did not carefully observe. "He is," said the cura, "one of the guardians of the tapadas. He is more than a hundred years old. He was, with Tupac Amaru when he undertook to overturn the Spanish power, and he led the Aymaras when they sacked the town of Huancane, and slew every white man, woman, and child that fell into their hands. He is a Gentile still, and throws coca on the apachetas. Ah! if I only knew what that old man knows of the tapadas, Señor," exclaimed the cura with fervor, "I should not waste my life among these barbarians! You can pity me! And for the love of God, Señor, if you come across the treasures, share them with me! I can't live much longer here!" And the padre burst into a maudlin paroxysm of tears.

Von Tschudi, when he was at Tiahuanaco, found or obtained some ancient relics—small stone idols, if I remember rightly—but had not proceeded many miles on his way to La Paz before he was surrounded by a party of Indians from the town and compelled to surrender them. We suffered no molestation, although there is no doubt we were closely watched, and that the deaf and apparently almost sightless old stone cutter was a spy on our actions.

I have already said that our visit to Tiahuanaco was coincident in time with the chuño, or potato feast, and Holy Week. The population of the place, as indeed of the whole region, is Indian, the white priests, officials, and landed proprietors being so few as hardly to deserve enumeration. These Indians are of the Aymara as distinguished from the Quichua family, and are a swarthier, more sullen, and more cruel race. Their celebration of the chuño feast, a ceremony dating back of the Conquest, and of the feast of the Church, were equally remarkable, and as throwing some light on their earlier practices and present condition, probably not unworthy a brief notice.

I have mentioned an acrid variety of the potato as among the principal articles of food in the Sierra. It is rendered more palatable than when used in its natural state, and better capable of being preserved, by being spread out on the ground, and exposed for some weeks to the frosts at night and the sun by day, until it becomes chuño, when it is stored away for consumption. The chuño had just been housed when we reached Tiahuanaco; and on the second night after our arrival the preparations for celebrating the event were commenced—commenced by large indulgences in chicha and cañaso, with corresponding uproars in different parts of the village, strangely compounded of cheers, howls, whoops, and shrieks, not favorable to sleep, and not altogether assuring to travelers among a people notoriously morose, jealous, and vindictive. On the morning of our third day, as we started out for the ruins, we noticed that the sides of the plaza were lined with vendors of chicha, chupe, coarse cakes, and charqui, or jerked meat, and that several posts had been erected in various parts of the square. During the day the bells of the church clanged incessantly; there was an irregular fusillade of cohetas (diminutive, spiteful rockets), and an unceasing drumming, relieved, or at any rate varied, by the shrill notes of the syrinx, or Pan's pipe, and the wild, savage shouts of the revelers.

Headdress of Indian Female Dancers

80

I shall never forget the extraordinary scene that startled us on our return to the village in the evening. The streets were deserted, and the entire population of the place was gathered in the plaza, grouped along its sides, where glowed fires fed by stalks of quinua; while the central part of the square was occupied by four groups of male and female dancers, dressed in ordinary costume except that the men in each group had handkerchiefs, or squares of cotton cloth of different colors, fastened, as a distinguishing badge, over their right shoulders, and falling down their backs. They wore headdresses of various colored feathers or plumes, lengthened out by slips of tame, and rising to the height of from five to six feet, like an inverted umbrella, from a headband tightly fitting around the forehead. Under the left arm each man held a rude drum, large in circumference but shallow, which he beat with a stick grasped in his right hand, while in his left he held to his mouth a Pan's pipe, differing in size and tone from that of his neighbor. With each group were a number of females, all dressed in blue, but, like the men, wearing scarfs of differently colored cloth over their left shoulders crossing their breasts. They, too, wore singular hats or headdresses, of stiff paper, the rim perfectly flat and round, plaited and cut so as to represent the conventional figure of the sun with its rays. The crown was composed of three semicircular pieces, placed triangularly, with the rays, in different colors, radiating from little square mirrors set in their centre.

Each group danced vigorously to its united music, which made up in volume what it lacked in melody—wild and piercing, yet lugubrious; the shrill pipe and the dull drum, with frequent blasts on cows' horns, by amateurs, among the spectators. Every man seemed anxious to excel his neighbor in the energy of his movements, which were often extravagant; but the motions of the women were slow and stately. The music had its cadences, and its emphatic parts were marked by corresponding emphatic movements in the dance. The "devilish music" that Cortez heard after his first repulse before Mexico, lasting the livelong night, and which curdled his blood with horror, while his captured companions were sacrificed to Huitzlipochtli—the Aztec war god—could not be stranger or more fascinating, more weird or savage, than that which rung in our ears during the rest of our stay in Tiahuanaco. All night and all day, still the festival went on, growing wilder and noisier, and only culminating when the feast of the Church commenced. It was an extraordinary spectacle, that of the symbols of Christianity and the figures of our Saviour and the saints carried by a reeling priest and staggering Indians through the streets of Tiahuanaco, while the chuño revelers danced and drummed around them. The chants of the Church were mingled with the sharp tones of the syrinx while the bells pealed, and the foul smoke of wretched candles combined with the odor of damp powder obscured and poisoned the atmosphere. In the church, before the dim altar, when the Host was raised in the unsteady hands of the sot who affronted Heaven and debased religion, the saturnalia reached its height, and we left the scene, with a clear conviction that the savage rites of the Aymaras had changed in name only, and that the festival we had witnessed was a substantial rehearsal of ceremonies and observances antedating the Discovery.

The road northward from Tiahuanaco is raised above the general level in consequence of the flooding of the plain during the rainy season, and marked every league by adobe columns. Passing some large buildings, situated at the base of the western hills, which had belonged to the Jesuits, who obtained and at one time held almost absolute control of this entire region, and reared in every village temples emulating in massiveness those of the Incas, we reached, at a distance of four leagues, the village of Guaque, distinguished not alone for its vast church, but for containing in its plaza half a dozen quenua or wild olive trees, with trunks at least five inches in diameter—isolated and, in this part of the Sierra, mammoth products of the vegetable world. Here, too, the Indians were celebrating Holy Week, but instead of the syrinx they played on a kind of flute of cane; their drums were smaller, and their headdresses different from those of their neighbors of Tiahuanaco, but quite as gaudy. They wore similar insignia over their shoulders, but were not so utterly gone in intoxication.

A little beyond Guaque the road strikes the shore of the Lake of Titicaca, or rather the lesser body of water connected with it, and sometimes called Tiquini or Chucuito. For a considerable distance from the shore the water is shallow, and is full of a kind of lake weed which grows to the surface, where it forms an evergreen mat. This weed is freely eaten by the oxen and cows of the Sierra, and is their principal food when drouth and frost destroy the pasturage. They wade into the water until their backs are scarcely visible in order to obtain it, advancing further and further from shore as the lake level falls, so that there is always a clear space of water near the land, and an emerald belt of verdure beyond. According to the Darwinian theory the cows around Titicaca must in time become hippopotami.

All along, overhanging the road and the lake shore, is a cliff of red sandstone, great blocks of which have fallen down and obstruct the path. This stone is precisely the same with many of the blocks in the ruins of Tiahuanaco, and the latter were no doubt obtained from some portion of the great ledge under the shadow of which we traveled.

Cattle Feeding on Lake Weed, Lake Titicaca

Five leagues from Guaque and nine from Tiahuanaco we reached the Desaguadero a second time. It forms here the boundary between Bolivia and Peru, and each state has a customs establishment and a dozen soldiers on its own bank. One of these peremptorily ordered us up to the tumble down building which bears the name of Aduana; but the officer in command, who had heard of our approach, permitted us to pass on without dismounting.

Totora Bridge Over the Outlet of Lake Titicaca

We crossed the river at the point where it debouches from the lake, on another floating bridge of totora. A few balsas of the same material were moored just above the bridge, as was also a rough wooden barge, sloop rigged, built at great expense by Mr. Forbes, for transporting hither copper ores from the opposite shore of the lake. The river flows out through a low and marshy plain, bounded by high disrupted cliffs of lime and sandstone, with a strong, majestic current. After a course of a few miles it spreads out in a series of shallow lakes or marshes, totorales, full of reeds, fish, and waterfowls, in which the remnants of a wild Indian tribe, the Uros, have their abodes. They live on floats or rafts of totora, and, it is alleged, subsist on fish and game, cultivating only a few bitter potatoes and ocas in the recesses of the Sierra of Tiahuanaco. *[These Indians and their modes of life are mentioned by Herrara in his History. "They were so savage," he affirms, "that when asked who they were, they answered they were not men but Uros, as if they had been a different species of animals. In the lake (of Titicaca) there were found whole towns of them living on floats of totora, made fast to rocks, and when they thought fit the whole town removed to another place." This illustration of the modes of life of a rude, primitive people has interest in connection with the discovery of the remains of what are called "lacustrine" dwellings in the Swiss lakes.]*

The village called El Desaguadero is built on the Peruvian bank of the river, under the shadow of a high rocky eminence, on which stand, the gray ruins of an old Calvario or church. The village is mean, with a dilapidated, half roofed church in the plaza, of which the cura and principal inhabitants were enjoying the fiesta. Across the entrance of the plaza, stretched between two crooked poles, was a rope, from which depended what were meant to be decorations. These consisted chiefly of silver valuables belonging to the people— cups, goblets, plates, platters, soup tureens, spoons, strings of Spanish dollars, and one or two articles of domestic use which will hardly bear to be designated, and which certainly, whether of silver or other material, are seldom conspicuous in well-conducted households. In the corners of the plaza were improvised altars adorned with mirrors, paintings from the church, highly colored lithographs, and gay hangings, such as bedspreads, scarlet tablecloths, variegated sashes and handkerchiefs, and other flaming finery. To the left of the plaza was a kind of open tent or awning spread over a space carpeted with a mat of reeds, within which were seats, and here was the elite of the place, of both sexes, engaged in celebrating the fiesta, while some Indians, fantastically dressed, were dancing to discordant music in front of the little church.

The scene was equally droll and barbaric, and we involuntarily checked our horses as we passed beneath the extraordinary string of treasures that garnished the entrance to the plaza. We had hardly time to take in the view before we were approached by the cura himself, holding in one hand a bottle and in the other a small silver cup. His face was red and glistening, his eyes watery and blinking, his step decidedly unsteady, and his accents thick. He insisted on our taking a trago, and then on our dismounting, and being introduced to the party beneath the awning, where, in answer to our inquiries, he said we would find the commandante, to whom we had letters, and on whose hospitality we proposed to trespass. So we complied, and were formally introduced to each and all of the caballeros and señoritas—for it is the custom to designate all the women of Peru, young and old, married and single, by this diminutive designation. And with each and all we had to take a tragito, happily in cups not much bigger than a thimble. The senoritas were certainly affable and the gentlemen almost affectionate—it was late in the afternoon, and this was the third day of the fiesta—so that we had some difficulty in getting away with the commandante to his house, which, like all the others, was small and poor. The commandante was an old man, and yet only a colonel, in a country where every third man is a general, and every tenth one a grand marshal. He, nevertheless, claimed a historic name and relationship with the last of the viceroys.

Grand Entry Into the Pueblo of El Desaguardero

I shot some ducks in the half-frozen pools behind the commandante's house, and what with these, some articles from my stores, and a mess of a very good fish called suches, from the lake (the sole contribution of the commandante), we did not sup altogether badly in El Desaguadero. My bed was spread on a settle of rough poles on one side of the room, under which the dishes from our table were hustled away by the solitary Indian pongo or servant —for such a thing as cleansing the cups and plates for the next meal until the time for the next meal comes round is unknown in Peru. H — contrived to dispose himself on some bags of barley in a corner, and the commandante, under the hallucination consequent on three days of festivities, mistook my wax candles for his fetid dips, and disappeared with them, two boxes of sardines, and a can of biscuits, in another apartment. I fear he was not an early riser, for he had not made his appearance when we left in the morning.

Climbing the abrupt ridge behind the town of El Desaguadero, we descended again to the shore, of the lake, along which the road runs to the town of Zepita, a rambling, shabby place, hanging on the skirts of a long and steep ridge just above a low, marshy plain. We found here a kind of tambo, in which were gathered a great number of drunken natives, returning from the fair of Vilque, near Puno, and were obliged to breakfast on the tough flesh of a veteran llama that had been killed that morning, eked out with a few eggs. Mule meat, especially from an animal that has been killed because he is too much reduced to travel, is not highly esteemed by epicures, but I can testify that it is preferable to that of the llama in its best estate.

At Zepita we turned off from the direct road to Puno to the right, over the marshy plain of which I have spoken, for the purpose of visiting the Peninsula of Copacabana, and the island adjacent. The path runs on a causeway of earth and stones that keeps it above the pools and creeks of the low plain, over which were scattered great flocks of water fowls of almost every kind, including vast numbers of gulls, white and mottled, flamingoes, ibises, geese, ducks, water hens, and divers. These would whirl up in clouds, with a noise like that of a high wind in a forest, on our approach, and circle screaming in the air, and then settle down again on some new spot, literally hiding the ground from sight. The bridges across the water runways are curious constructions of turf, each layer projecting over that beneath until the upper ones touch and brace against each other, forming a rude kind of arch. Curious, but not calculated to inspire any strong sense of security. The absence of wood and timber has led the people of the Sierra to adopt a great many novel and striking devices to remedy the deficiency; in architecture and navigation as well as in road making.

At the distance of a league the ground becomes higher and firm, sloping gently to the south, and dotted over with houses and flocks. Nowhere in the interior of Peru does the traveler find more evidences of industry and thrift than here. The wealth of the people consists almost entirely in herds and flocks. They supply La Paz and Arequipa with cattle and produce a valuable annual crop of wool. Owing to some advantage in exposure, better soil, or fortunate reaction of the lake on the temperature, they raise the best potatoes of the region, and in some favorable seasons their barley will mature.

In all directions over the undulating slope are numberless mounds of stone heaped together with great regularity—the result, probably, of ages of labor in clearing the stony ground. We observed also, lying near our path; many large blocks of basalt and trachyte, some completely and others only partially hewn, and corresponding exactly in material and workmanship with those at Tiahuanaco. They were evidently obtained from the quarries visible at the foot of the rocky eminences on our left, and abandoned midway to the lake. I have no doubt that most if not all the stones at Tiahuanaco were procured here, and from the sandstone cliffs south of El Desaguadero, and were transported on floats, or balsas, to the southern extremity of the bay of Guaqui.

All day we enjoyed a magnificent panorama of the great bulk of Illampu and its snow crowned dependencies, which appeared to rise from the very edge of the bright blue lake, itself dotted with bold, brown islands. At five o'clock we reached Yunguyo, situated on the narrow isthmus that connects the peninsula of Copacabana with the mainland. It is a considerable town, with two large churches and a great plaza, which we found full of drunken, noisy revelers, who, the night before, had succeeded in setting fire to the thatched roof of a pulperia, whence the flames had spread around two sides of the square, leaving only a series of low, black walls, within which still steamed up a choking smoke and a sickening odor of smouldering damp hay and burning feathers. The "conflagration" had not checked the humors of the fiesta, and drumming and piping and dancing were going on with an energy only equaled by that displayed at

Tiahuanaco. We had some difficulty in getting through the boisterous and rather sinister looking crowd, and still more in finding anybody sober enough to show us the house of the commandante. He was out, attending a grand dinner of the authorities of the place, reinforced by the presence of the district judge from Juli; but he no sooner heard of our arrival than he left his friends and hastened to welcome us, and then insisted on our returning with him and joining the festive party. It was in vain we protested that we were unpresentable in polite society, and begged to be allowed to change our coarse and travel stained clothing.

We were literally captured by our new and ardent friend, and followed him submissively to the banquet. The gathering was chiefly of men dressed in black, which is severe *au regle* on grand occasions in Peru. But the styles were various, extending through those of many years. And the stove pipe hats —well, I couldn't help thinking that they had been borrowed from some Hebraic receptacle of that tasteful covering for the head. The ladies were dressed in a garb less foreign and less pretentious, but much more tasteful and appropriate. Chupe, in a variety of shapes, and different degrees of consistency and nauseousness, formed the staple of the dinner, while the "flowing bowl" was, filled with sweet Malaga wine with a distinct flavor of treacle and sienna. Abundant wild fowl, geese and ducks of many varieties, were disporting within gunshot of our windows, and fish were eager to be caught within a hundred paces, yet we had neither fish nor game, only chupe and lean mutton of the color and nearly of the consistence of blocks of mahogany.

It is a fashion, not confined to Yunguyo, to select delicate morsels from your own plate and pass them on your fork to any lady to whom you may feel disposed to be attentive. The lady can with propriety respond; and it is the height of condescension, and a special compliment, if she reciprocates the attention by placing the morsel in your mouth with her own fingers. It is a little startling at first, and, on the whole, not a fashion likely to spread very far beyond the limits of Peru.

The lion of the day was the legal luminary and judicial functionary of Juli. He was misplaced in the Sierra, and only required to have had cheeks a little more puffy, a voice a trifle more grum, and a horse hair wig to have made him an ornament to the English bench. He was familiar with Roman Law and the Code Napoleon, but rather weak in geography, and somewhat confused as to the relative positions of London and New York. On his earnest solicitation I promised to stop with him when I reached Juli— whereof more in another place.

A Dinner Compliment in Yunguyo

The boundary between Peru and Bolivia—a most arbitrary and inconvenient one—crosses the isthmus leading to the Peninsula of Copacabana, a league beyond Yunguyo. Among the guests at our dinner was the Bolivian commandante of the Peninsula; and we arranged to leave our baggage mules behind to recuperate, and to accompany him next morning to the seat of his jurisdiction, where the famous Virgin of Copacabana has her rich and imposing shrine. Thence we proposed to visit the Sacred Islands of Titicaca.

THE SACRED ISLANDS.

Shrine of Nuestra Senora de Copacabana, Bolivia

A LEAGUE past Yunguyo the traveler ascends a high transverse ridge, which is the boundary between Bolivia and Peru. Just within the line, and in the territory of the latter, stands the Calvario of Yunguyo, half church half fortress, which is the Peruvian bulwark against Bolivian invasion by way of the Peninsula of Copacabana.

Beyond the church militant is a sweet vale, circled in by rocks of fantastic form, which it requires but little imagination to shape into rigid and monstrous figures of men and animals. And I could well understand how the pilgrim in Inca times, wending his weary way to the Sacred Islands, might have his simple and superstitious mind impressed and awed by these stony effigies, which tradition says are the vestiges of impious men and giants whom an outraged divinity had congealed into stone, as a punishment for their iniquities and a warning to those who might follow them over this holy path without

91

due preliminary fasting and penitential propitiations.

Climbing another ridge which shoots out abruptly into the lake from the high, rocky, central mass of the peninsula, and passing some fields of oca and patches of lupins, we came to a spot, marked by the ruins of an ancient church, where the Bay of Copacabana is first seen spreading out its blue tranquil waters, framed in by rugged headlands, and lending its liquid perspective to the Island of Titicaca, sacred to the beneficent Sun, and on which first fell the footsteps of his celestial messenger. I am an old traveler, and not given to "sensations," but I must confess that here I experienced an emotion. At least I was so assured by H—, who felt my pulse for the purpose of ascertaining the fact. "Deducting for a slight irregularity, consequent on walking up the hill rather rapidly, he discovered a percussion in the pulse, such as often attends sudden excitement." And he recommended a tranquilizing glass of chicha from the stores with which Berrios had been supplied by the considerate commandante of Yunguyo. Satisfied with his diagnosis of my case, and accepting the remedy, I walked along the crest of the ridge to the point where it broke off in a sheer cliff, two thousand feet perpendicular, and occupied myself in timing the fall of stones into the water below, while H— made a sketch of the scene.

View of the Bay of Copacabana, Lake Titicaca, Bolivia

Down the steep declivity of the ridge, between substantial stone walls defining fields just cleared of their barley, or in which quaintly dressed Indians were gathering the bright and tender ocas, we finally turned the point of a promontory, and came in view of the Ciudad Bendita of Copacabana—a large and rambling town, built on an eminence at the base of a pyramid of lofty, splintered rocks, with the gray and solemn mass of the Shrine of Nuestra Señora de Copacabana rising grandly in the centre of its low and clustering habitations, just as the Cathedral of Strasbourg and the Duomo of Milan project their stately outlines above the haunts of men at their feet.

Minor shrines there were in the suburbs, gaudy in archaic coloring, in which pilgrims through prayer and penance prepare themselves to encounter the greater sanctities in store for them in the sacred village. Our commandante did not mind the shrines, but ordered up the first inhabitant he met, who removed his hat, touched his forehead to our stirrups, saluting us with "Tattai Viracocha," and directed him, in Aymara, to prepare some house that he designated for our reception, and to get barley for our animals. Clearly the commandante knew how to use his powers in Copacabana!

Nothing could be drearier than the streets of the seat of the famous Virgin. The houses are as close and repulsive as those of Tiahuanaco. The plaza is wide, but the buildings on three sides are dwarfed by the imposing architectural proportions of the shrine occupying the remaining side. The fiesta of the church was nearly over, and the candles had flared out and the flowers were withered in the improvised shrines or altars that had been raised under makeshift tents in the corners of the plaza. A line of Aymara women, each with her little store of aji, ocas, dried fish, lupins, or charqui, was ranged down the centre of the square, while a vagrant herd of thin, bow backed dogs sneaked over the vacant space in hopeless search for some fragment of food to satiate their ravenous hunger. Squalid Indians and lean llamas glided around the corners, and shivering, unkempt Indian women glanced out furtively from behind the hide curtains that answer for doors of their wretched dwellings, as we clattered over the rough stone pavements toward the house of the commandante. Squalor of life was never more strongly contrasted with splendor in religion than in this remote and almost inaccessible town of Copacabana.

The house of the commandante was by no means imposing, his retinue was not grand, and his menage was scant, but when we rode under the low and crumbling archway that led to the courtyard of his modest residence his retainers hastened, with uncovered heads, to touch their foreheads to our knees, and to hail us "Tattai Viracochar —Father Viracocha—for Viracocha, born of the sea, and one of the most conspicuous personages of the Inca pantheon, had blue eyes, fair hair, and a light complexion. They did not salute our dark browed and sallow host with any such appellation, and he was evidently a little annoyed by the omission, since he asked us to pardon los tontos, "the idiots!" We were vain enough not to see the matter in the same light with the commandante, and H— was at a loss to know "why a blue eyed Irishman and a fair haired Yankee should require to have an apology because they happened to be mistaken for demi-gods." In fact, we only regretted that we did not possess a first rate huaca and a moderate knowledge of Aymara, to enable us to set up an opposition establishment to that of Nuestra Señora, on the hill opposite to her gorgeous temple. For the sanctity of Copacabana is by no means wholly due to Nuestra Señora, but rather to a certain "idol of vast renown among the gentiles," that preceded her here, to whom, the chroniclers tell us, were raised "sumptuous temples," and who was attended by "a multitude of priests and virgins."

The commandante secured us a vacant house, which from having been long shut up was a little close and musty, but as four months had passed since its occupants had died of smallpox it was considered safe for Viracochas. And he gave us a breakfast as sumptuous as utter disregard of expense and a reckless exercise of unrestricted authority could secure. A pig had been slain and paid for, but there was an Aymara household, like Rachel, comfortless and in tears, for it could not be replaced—there were only four more in all Copacabana! And the commandante exulted in producing a pound of Puno butter, golden under its transparent covering. Then we had ocas boiled and ocas roasted to eat with the butter withal. Still, crescendo, we had onions, small, it is true, but very strong; and I capped the topmost wave of our morning of enjoyment by producing a box of biscuits, crisp as when they came from the defty hand of the London baker. Chicha was not altogether a successful substitute for Falernian, but then all deficiencies were more than made up by a cup of Yungas coffee, fragrant and potential, a fortification and solace to the body, and a stimulus to the intelligence.

Any description of the church and shrine of Nuestra Señora of Copacabana would convey but a poor idea of its extent and magnificence. It is built mainly of brick, roofed with glistening tiles, and stands within a vast square surrounded by heavy walls and planted with quenua trees and the shrub that produces the brilliant crimson trumpet shaped flower called Flor del Inca (Cantuta buxifolia). The entrance is through ponderous iron gates, wrought in Spain, beneath a lofty gateway. In the inclosure fronting the church is a majestic dome of stone, ninety feet high, rising over three tall and elaborately carved crosses of berenguela, supported on a graduated base of the same material. Sculptured figures of saints and angels bend down from the cornice, and the mystic triangle appears in the midst of a painted glory in the dome. At each corner of the court are square substantial structures of brick, closed by solid iron doors, and without other opening except one or two narrow portholes. In these are deposited the bones of the pilgrims who have died at Copacabana.

The church is high, and the interior so sombre that it is with difficulty one can make out the elaborate ornaments of the various altars and the subjects of the numerous pictures that cover its walls. Connected with it are courts and cloisters, sown with barley or choked with rubbish, the crazy doors creaking dismally on their hinges, and all things suggestive of decay and desolation.

The great feature of the edifice, however, is the camarin of the Virgin, which is a large room behind the great altar. Here is her shrine, and this is the Holy of Holies of Copacabana. Admittance here must be prefaced by confession and the payment of a certain sum of money. In this way the revenues of Nuestra Señora are kept up, and her corps of priests supported. The guardian of the shrine, a handsome, intelligent man from La Paz, on whose shoulders the mantle of the priesthood rested lightly, and who appeared better fitted for the camp and the forum than the services of the altar, received us in the ante room of the camarin, and with a smile made a dispensation of both fee and confession in our favor. The camarin is reached by two stairways, one for ascent on one side and another for descent on the other, so that the crowds that pay their devotions here at stated periods may not come to an absolute deadlock. The fiesta had drawn together a considerable number of Indians from the neighboring towns, and an unbroken line of them was ascending the stairs, the stone steps of which were deeply worn by pious knees, guided by a priest who, seated in a niche, drawled out certain chants or prayers in Aymara, which were responded to by the devotees. Our conductor ordered the dusky pilgrims peremptorily to make room for us, and they flattened themselves against the rough walls on either side that we might pass. The camarin or chamber of the Virgin is judiciously draped so as to secure only that "dim, religious light" of which poets write. A thick but rather gaudy carpet covered the floor, a cabinet organ stood in a niche near the door, and the walls were covered with votive offerings of every kind and every degree of value. Here were the diamond hilted sword and the gold mounted pistols of General Santa Cruz, and the jewels of his wife, as well as little rude silver representations of arms, legs, hearts, and eyes, deposited here by the Indians in token of the wonderful interpositions and cures of Nuestra Señora.

Seats Cut in the Rock at Copacabanoa

The image of the Virgin is kept in a kind of alcove, behind a heavy curtain of embroidered velvet, and shut off from too close approach by a stout silver railing. At the tinkling of a bell by some unseen acolyte, who next struck up a monotonous strain on the parlor organ, everybody sunk on his knees, the spangled velvet veil was slowly withdrawn, and the milagrosa imagen of Nuestra Señora of Copacabana revealed to our heretical eyes. It is an elaborately dressed figure, scarcely three feet high, brilliant in gay satins, and loaded with gold and jewels. Its head is a mite in comparison with the blazing crown that it supports, and its face is delightfully white and pink, and as glistening as the average of female busts in the windows of the shops of metropolitan *coiffeurs des dames*. It derives special celebrity and no doubt much of its popularity among the Indians from the fact that it was made, so runs the legend, in 1582 by Tito-Yupanqui, a lineal descendant of the ruling Incas, who had had no previous instruction in art, but who was inspired by the Virgin herself, who favored him with a special sitting, so that there should be no mistake in her portrait.

This shrine is the resort of pilgrims from almost every part of Catholic America, but especially from the provinces of Brazil and the La Plata. As many as thirty thousand have been known to visit it in a single season. Nor is the renown of Our Lady of Copacabana limited to America. Among the suffering faces of the devotees in the camarin I shall never forget that of a fair, pale girl who was reclining on a mat in front of the shrine, with her great lustrous eyes fixed immovably on the image of the Virgin. Every day for weeks she had been lifted to her place in the sacred chamber. She was from Barcelona, in Spain, and had come here as a last resort, after having visited every shrine of celebrity in the Old World.

Around the neck of the image of the Virgin were several strings of little wooden crosses, one of which the custodian reverently removed, and placed it in my hand as we descended the stairs. It is supposed to have imbibed special virtues and powers from having been hung around the neck of the Virgin for one single night. We saw and listened in decorous silence, but on our way with our conductor to his apartments, under his invitation to join him in a glass of sherry, H—profanely observed that, except the convent at the foot of Mount Sinai, he knew of no place fiat would better repay the sacking than the shrine of Nuestra Señora of Copacabana. The guardian's eyes twinkled when I repeated to him the impious observation, and he gave me an answer which in its ambiguity led me to infer that the conservators of the shrine had long before taken judicious care of all the real diamonds and rubies that had been deposited there by pious penitents, and that the loot of the robber of the camarin would hardly repay him for his risks of detection in this world and damnation in the next.

The "Bath of the Incas," Copacabana

The idol that lent its sanctity and fame to Copacabana, before it was supplanted by the handiwork of Tito-Yupanqui, also gave its name to the place and peninsula; the word signifying, according to the chroniclers, a precious stone from which one may see, or which gives vision. It was buried by the Indians on the arrival of the Spaniards, but subsequently disinterred by the latter and broken in pieces. It was of a beautiful blue stone, representing the human face. The temples of which the early writers speak have entirely disappeared, or left only few and unsatisfactory traces. Yet in the suburbs of the town, near the cemetery, we find a great number of niches, steps, and what appear to have been intended as seats cut in the rocks, which may have had some connection with the ancient worship. At the hacienda of Cusijata, half a league from the town, there are some scant remains of what tradition affirms was a palace of the Incas. These consist mainly of large and well cut blocks of stone; but the sole remaining object of interest is what is called "the Bath of the Inca." It may be described as a huge vase of simple form, cut from a single block of fine grained trachyte, having an inner diameter of three feet four inches, and a depth of five feet two inches. Its walls are six inches thick. It is now sunk in the ground, in a small, dilapidated building of adobes, and is still used as a bath.

View From The "Ladera," Island of Titicaca in the Distance

Immediately on our arrival in Copacabana the commandant had sent an Indian with an order to the alcaldes of the island of Titicaca to have a balsa in readiness for on the following day at the embarcadero of Yampupata, four leagues distant. We started for that point at noon, with the intention of reaching the island the same night. The road descends abruptly from the rocky eminence on which the town is built into a beautiful level amphitheatre two miles broad, and curves around the head of a bay that here projects into the land between two high and rugged capes. The water toyed and sparkled among the pebbles on the shore, and along it a troop of lively plover was racing in eager search for the minute mollusks drifted up by the waves, with the advance and recession of which their line kept a wavering cadence. Past the little plain is what in Peru is called a ladera; in other words, the road runs high up along the face of the steep, and in many places absolutely perpendicular, headlands that overhang the lake, and becomes a mere goat's path, narrow and rugged, half worn half cut in the rock. But neither the difficulty nor danger of the path could wholly withdraw our attention from the hundreds of wide and wonderful views that burst on our sight at every bend and turning. The bold bare peninsulas, the bluff panoramic headlands behind which the lake stole in through many a rent in their rocky palisade, and spread out in broad and placid bays, the islands equally abrupt and bold and bare, the ruddy bulk of the sacred island of Titicaca, the distant shores of Bolivia, with their silver cincture of the Andes, the blue waters and sparkling waves, with almost every other element of the beautiful and impressive, went to make up the kaleidoscopic scenes of the afternoon, and with the cloudless sky, bright sunlight, and bracing air, to inspire us with a sense of elevation and repose inconsistent with the babbling of waters, the rustle of leaves, and the murmurs of men.

Beyond the ladera we came once more to the pebbly shore of the lake; then climbing the steep neck of a rocky peninsula, and skirting the cultivated slopes of a gentle declivity, between walls of stone inclosing fields of ocas which, newly dug, shone like gems on the gray earth, we descended to the embarcadero of Yampupata. Here is a sandy beach between rocky promontories, and a tambo of stone, windowless, and with but a single opening into its bare interior, black with smoke, floored with ashes, and redolent of indescribable and offensive odors. There was no balsa to convey us to the island, which lay glowing in the evening sun temptingly before us, and appearing through the moistureless air as if scarcely at rifle shot distance. We hurried to a group of huts clustered round a little church a mile to our left, but most of the population was absent in Copacabana or at work in the oca fields, and we learned little from the blind, the halt, and the deaf that remained behind, except that balsas would come for us from the island. Through our glasses we could discover a number of these moored in little rock girt coves and indentations of its shores, but there was nobody near them, nor sign of life whatever. In vain as night fell we lighted fierce and ephemeral fires of quenua stalks; our signals were unanswered, and we were obliged to dispose ourselves for the night in the cold and gloomy tambo.

Balsa Navigation on Lake Titicaca

I was up at daylight and went down to the shore, where the lake weed was matted together with ice, and where a group of Indian women were awaiting shiveringly the arrival of a balsa which I discerned just paddling out from under the shadow of the island. Although apparently so near, the balsa was several hours in crossing the strait, and it was ten o'clock before it ranged up alongside and under the protection, of some rocks to the left of the tambo. It was small, water soaked, and its highest part elevated only a few inches above the water. The Indian women endeavored to get aboard, but a personage in a poncho, and evidently in authority, for he carried a tasseled cane, forbade them. He approached us hat in hand, with the usual salutation of Tattai Viracocha, and announced himself as curaca of Titicaca, at our service. Berrios declined to embark on the balsa, which, to start with, was a ticklish craft, and with H—, myself, the alcalde, and the two boatmen, barely kept afloat.

Now sailing in a balsa is by no means the perfection of navigation, nor is the craft itself one likely to inspire high confidence. It is simply a float or raft made up of bundles of reeds, tied together fagot like, in the middle of which the voyager poises himself on his knees, while the Indian marineros stand one at each extremity, where they spread their feet apart, and with small and rather crooked poles for oars strike the water right and left, and thus slowly and laboriously propel the balsa in the required direction. Of course this action gives the craft a rocking, rolling motion, and makes the passenger feel very much as if he were afloat on a mammoth cigar, predisposed to turn over on the slightest pretext. Then if the water be a little rough, a movement takes place which probably is unequaled in bringing on the pleasant sensation of seasickness. Some of the balsas, however, are large, with sides built up like guards, which can be rigged with a sail for running before the wind, and are capable of carrying as many as sixty people.

Leaving the little playa or beach behind, our Indian boatmen pushed along under a steep rocky cliff until they reached the point where the strait between the mainland and the island is narrowest. The water at the foot of the cliff is very deep, but wonderfully transparent, and we could trace the plunge downward of the precipitous limestone buttresses until our brains grew dizzy.

We were upward of two hours in propelling the balsa across the strait, a distance which an ordinary oarsman, in a Whitehall boat would get over in fifteen minutes, and landed on the island under the lee of a projecting ledge of rocks, full in view of the Palace of the Inca and the terraces surrounding it, half a mile to our right.

I do not think I shall find a better place than this for saying a few words about Lake Titicaca, which is to be for many weeks a conspicuous feature in our landscape, and which is in many respects the most extraordinary and interesting body of water in the world. It is a long irregular oval in shape, with one-fifth of its area at its southern extremity cut nearly off by the opposing peninsulas of Tiquina and Copacabana. Its greatest length is about 120 miles, and its greatest width between 50 and 60 miles. Its mean level is 12,864 feet above the sea. The eastern or Bolivian shore is abrupt, the mountains on that side pressing down boldly into the water. The western and southern shores, however, are relatively low and level, the water shallow and grown up with reeds and rushes, among which myriads of water fowls find shelter and support.

The lake never freezes over, but ice forms near its shores and where the water is shallow. In fact it exercises a very important influence on the climate of this high, cold, and desolate region. Its waters, at least during the winter months, are from 10 to 12 degrees of Fahrenheit warmer than the atmosphere. The islands and peninsulas feel this influence most perceptibly, and I found barley, pease, and maize, the latter, however, small and not prolific, ripening on these, while they did not mature on what may be called the mainland. The prevailing winds are from the northeast, and they often blow with great force, rendering navigation on the frail balsas, always slow and difficult, exceedingly dangerous.

The lake has several considerable bays, of which those of Puno, Huancane, and Achacache are the principal. It has also eight considerable habitable islands, viz.: Amantene, Taqueli, Soto, Titicaca, Coati, Campanario, Toquaré, and Aputo. Of these the largest is that of Titicaca, on which we have just landed; high and bare, rugged in outline as rugged in surface, six miles long by between three and four in width.

This is the sacred island of Peru. To it the Incas traced their origin, and to this day it is held by their descendants in profound veneration. According to tradition, Manco Capac and his wife and sister Mama Oella, children of the Sun and commissioned by that luminary, started hence on their errand of beneficence to reduce under government and to instruct in religion and the arts the savage tribes that occupied the country. Manco Capac bore a golden rod, and was instructed to travel northward until he should reach the spot where the rod should sink into the ground, and there fix the seat of his empire. He obeyed the behest, traveled slowly along the western shore of the lake, through the broad, level Puna lands, up the Valley of the Pucura, to the Lake of La Raya, where the basin of Titicaca, ends, and whence the waters of the River Vilcanota start on their course to swell the Amazon. He advanced down the valley of that river until he reached the spot where Cuzco now stands, when the golden rod disappeared. Here he fixed his seat, and here in time rose the city of the Sun, the capital of the Inca empire— an empire larger than that of Adrian, grander than that of Charlemagne—which extended over more than 37 degrees of latitude, and from the eastern base of the Andes, where "Huge Orellano rolls his affluent flood," westward to where the great Pacific heaves its unavailing waves against the deeply planted feet of the Cordillera.

Upon this island, the traditional birthplace of the Incas, are still the remains of a temple of the Sun, a convent of priests, a royal palace, and other vestiges of Inca civilization. Not far distant is the Island of Coati, which was sacred to the Moon, the wife and sister of the Sun, on which stands the famous Palace of the Virgins of the Sun, built around two shrines dedicated to the Sun and the Moon respectively, and which is one of the best preserved as well as one of the most remarkable remains of aboriginal architecture on this continent. The Island of Soto was the Isle of Penitence to which the Incas of the ruling race were wont to resort for fasting and humiliation, and it has also many remains of ancient architecture.

Two alcaldes of the island, residing in the little village of Challa, were waiting on the rocks to receive us, which they did with uncovered heads and the usual salutation. They told us that they had mules ready for us beyond the rocks, up and through which we clambered by a steep and narrow path, worn in the stone by the feet of myriads of pilgrims. This leads to a platform faced with rough stones carefully laid, and reached by a flight of steps. Above this is another platform, ascended in like manner, on the further side of which are the remains of two rectangular buildings, each 35 feet long by 27 feet broad, with a narrow passage between them. The front of each building is much ruined, but relieved by re-entering niches of true Inca type and characteristic of Inca architecture. Midway from the passage between the buildings, which is only 30 inches wide, doors open into each edifice, which is composed of but a single room. The further sides of these have niches corresponding with those of the exterior. If there were any windows they were in the upper portions of the walls, now fallen. Both buildings are of blue limestone, roughly cut, and laid in a tough clay. They were probably stuccoed.

The purpose of these structures, or rather structure, is pretty well indicated by the early writers, who tell us that the pilgrims to the sacred island, after going through certain fasts, penances, and purifications in Copacabana, were permitted to visit the island, but on landing had to go, with many ceremonies and confessions, through three gates or doors—the door of the Puma, the door of the bird Kenti, and the gate of Hope—when they might continue their journey to the sacred rock.

Plan of Ancient Buildings at the Landing,
Island of Titcaca.

After making a rapid plan of these remains and of some works apparently fortifications on the declivity above, we mounted our mules, and with an alcalde trotting along in front of us and another behind, we started for the holy kaka or rock of Manco, and the convent of the ancient priests, at the opposite end of the island. The path skirts the flanks of the abrupt hills forming the island, apparently on the line of an ancient road supported by terraces of large stones, at an elevation of between two and three hundred feet above the lake, the shores of which are precipitous. At the distance of half a mile from the landing we passed a fine ruin called "The Palace of the Inca," and further on passed also "The Baths of the Inca," in a beautiful protected amphitheatre, irrigated by springs, yellow with ripening barley, and full of shrubs and flowers. Here the path turns to the right over the cumbre or crest of the Island, 2000 feet high, and runs along dizzy eminences, from which, far down, may be discerned little sheltered enseñadas or bays, almost landlocked, where there is a poor thatched hut or two, a balsa riding at her moorings or dragged up to dry on the shore, a few quenua trees, and whence comes up the sole music of the sierra, the bark, half yelp, half snarl of the ill conditioned, base tempered, but faithful dogs of the country. Sometimes our course was on one side of the crest, and sometimes on the other, so that we had alternating views of the Peruvian and Bolivian shores of the lake, and of the bays and promontories of the island.

At almost the very northern end of the island, at its most repulsive and unpromising part, where there is neither inhabitant nor trace of culture, where the soil is rocky and bare and the cliffs ragged and broken, high up where the eye ranges over the broad blue waters from one mountain barrier to the other, from the glittering crests of the Andes to those of the Cordillera, is the spot most celebrated and most sacred of Peru. Here is the rock on which it was believed no bird would light or animal venture, on which no human being dared to place his foot, whence the sun rose to dispel the primal vapors and illume the world, which was plated all over with gold and silver, and covered, except on occasions of the most solemn festivals, with a veil of cloth of richest color and material, which sheltered the favorite children of the Sun, and the pontiff, priest, and king who founded the Inca empire.

Our guides stopped when it came in view, removed their hats and bowed low and reverently in its direction, muttering a few words of mystic import. But this rock today—alas, for the gods dethroned is nothing more than a frayed and weather worn mass of red sandstone, part of a thick stratum that runs through the island, and which is here disrupted and standing with its associated shale and limestone layers, at an angle of 45° with the horizon. The part uncovered and protruding above the ground is about 225 feet long and 25 feet high. It presents a rough and broken and slightly projecting face, but behind subsides in a slope coinciding with the declivity of the eminence of which it is part. In the face are many shelves and pockets, all apparently natural. Excepting that there are traces of walls around it of cut stone, and that the ground in front is artificially leveled, there is nothing to distinguish it from many other projections of the sandstone strata on the island and the mainland. Calancha, one of the oldest chroniclers of this region, well observes that it has no special features to arrest the eye or fix the attention.

Niche in Ruins, the Landing, Island of TIticaca

Its position, however, is remarkable. It is on the crest of a ridge connecting with a bold promontory—a high, rocky mass with precipitous sides and dark, cavernous recesses, which forms the northern extremity of the island. On every side are bare rocks, heaped confusedly, except in front of the sacred stone itself, Where, as I have said, there is a level, artificial terrace 372 feet long and 125 feet broad, supported by a stonewall. At each outer corner of this terrace are the remains of small, square structures, probably those referred to by the chroniclers as the shrines of the thunder and lightning. According to tradition the earth of this terrace was brought from the distant rich and fertile valleys of the Amazonian rivers, so that it might nourish a verdure denied by the hard, ungrateful soil of the island.

From the front of this terrace the island falls off to the lake by a steep but smooth declivity, and the eye rests on the small but lovely bay of Chucaripe, in which the clear and sparkling waters ripple gently to a sandy shore, that contrasts pleasingly with the rugged cliffs rising on either hand. Black, rocky islets, frayed and shattered by earthquakes and storms, lift themselves up in the lake beyond; and away in the distance, sharply defined in the clear, rarefied atmosphere, are the hills of Juli and Pomata —the great church of the latter town gleaming out like a point of silver against the umber tinted background. Turning around and facing the sacred rock we find ourselves looking down on another similar bay or indentation, cliff bound, and in which the waves, driven by the keen northeast wind, dash and chafe angrily against the rocky shore, in striking contrast with the soft and almost slumberous repose of the opposing bay. This is called the Bay of Kentipunca, in which the Inca landed when he came to visit the spot sacred to the Sun. On a narrow natural platform half way down to the water are the remains of several structures, which were the residences, it is supposed, of priests and attendants. They are of rough stones, and not architecturally remarkable. From them, leading up to the shrine, is a broad road, partly hewn in the rock. About midway are what are called the "footprints of the Inca," revered among the Indians to this day, as indicating the place where Yupanqui stood when he made his pilgrimage to the island, and removed the imperial Ilautu from his forehead in token of submission and adoration of the divinity whose shrine rose before him. The so-called footprints certainly have a rough resemblance to the impression that might be produced by a sandaled foot; but they are rather large for those of even so mighty a personage as the Inca Yupanqui—being upward of three feet long and of corresponding width. They are formed, in outline, by hard, ferruginous veins around which the rock has been worn away, leaving them in relief.

It was in adoratorios or chapels here that the chroniclers affirm was placed the triune statue of stone, three figures united in one, which uncritical writers have made to do such large service, as evidence of the existence of the doctrine of the Trinity in Peru. These figures had names, so state the monkish authorities, signifying Great or Lord Sun, the Son of the Sun, and the Brother Son. Calancha thinks that the making the third person the brother of the first was a corruption of the mystery as taught by the apostles who came to America, and was suggested by the devil himself, so as to delude the ignorant natives to their spiritual ruin.

The Sacred Rock of Manco Capac

To the front and northward of the sacred rock, and distant about 200 paces, are the ruins of a large edifice which the chroniclers call the Despensa, or Storehouse of the Sun, but which is now called La Chingana, or The Labyrinth. It justifies the latter name. It is situated on the slope descending to the little bay of Chucaripe, at a point where the ground falls off very abruptly, so that its lower walls must have been twice or three times as high as those on its upper side. Its leading feature is a court, with terraces cut in the rock, and with a fountain in its centre. The walls facing inward on the court are all niched, and on each side are masses of buildings, which had evidently been two or three stories in height. Some of the lower rooms or vaults, probably all of them, had been arched after the manner to be observed in the "Palace of the Inca" at the opposite end of the island. The passages leading to the various rooms were narrow and intricate, the doorways low, and the rooms themselves small and dark, almost precluding the notion that they were intended to be inhabited. From its proximity to the rock, and the identity of its leading features with those of other structures of Peru of known purpose, I am inclined to regard the Chingana as one of the Aclahuasas or Houses of the Virgins of the Sun, one of which existed on the island, and I found no other building that could have served as a retreat for the vestals.

Pila, or Fountain of the Incas, Titicaca

The sun had set, casting a fleeting crimson glow on the snows of Illampu, which was followed by a deadly, bluish pallor, and it was beginning to be dark before we got through with our investigation of the rock of Manco Capac. We had arranged to pass the night at the little hacienda of the Pik or Bath of the Incas, and retraced our path thither slowly and with difficulty. The hacienda consisted of three small buildings, occupying as many sides of a court. One of these was a kitchen and dormitory, another was a kind of granary or storehouse, and in the third was an apartment reserved for the proprietor of the hacienda, a resident of Puno, when he visited the island. The room was neatly whitewashed, the floor was matted, and there were two real chairs from Connecticut, and a table that might be touched without toppling over, and used without falling in pieces. The alcaldes who had us in charge attended faithfully to our wants, and served us in person with chupe, ocas, and eggs. Their authority over the people of the hacienda seemed absolute.

The night was bitterly cold, and we had no covering except our saddle cloths, having declined the use of some sheep skins, which the alcaldes would have taken from the poor people of the establishment. A sheep skin, or the skin of the vicuña, spread on the mud floor of his hut is the only bed of the Indian from one year's end to the other. It is always filthy, and frequently full of vermin. Before going to bed we went out into the frosty, starry night, and were surprised to see fires blazing on the top most peak of the island, on the crest of Coati, and on the headland of Copacabana. Others, many of them hardly discernible in the distance, were also burning on the peninsula of Tiquina, and on the bluff Bolivian shores of the lake, their red light shimmering like golden lances over the water. Our first impression was that some mysterious signaling was going on, connected perhaps with our visit. We ascertained, however, that this was the Eve of St. John, which is celebrated in this way throughout the Sierra. On that night fires blaze on the hilltops in an the inhabited districts of Peru and Bolivia, from the desert of Atacama to the equator.

We were up early, and for the first time ate our chupe with satisfaction, for it was hot. We found the houses of the hacienda seated in the saddle of a ridge projecting into the lake, and terminating in a natural mound or eminence, rounded with great regularity by art, and terraced up to its top by concentric walls of stone. Traces of a building, like a belvedere or summer house, were conspicuous at its summit, from which a fine view of the lake, its islands, and the distant Nevadas is commanded. At the foot of this eminence, on both sides, are little bays with sandy beaches, that on the right pushing inland toward the terraced Garden of the Inca. Here is the most sheltered nook of the island, and the terraces are covered with barley in the ear, just changing from green to golden, and as we zig-zag down we come to patches of pease and little squares of maize, with stalks scarcely three feet high and ears not longer than one's finger, but closely covered with compact, vitreous grains. We go down, down, until we get where we hear the pleasant splash and gurgle of waters; there is an oppressive odor of fading flowers, and in a few minutes we stand before the Pila of the Incas. We are midway down the sloping valley, amidst terraces geometrically laid out and supported by walls of cut stone, niched according to Inca taste, and here forming three sides of a quadrangle, in which there is a pool, forty feet long, ten wide, and five deep, paved with worked stones. Into this pour four chorros or jets of water, each of the size of a man's arm, from openings cut in the stones behind. Over the walls around it droop the tendrils of vines and the stems of plants that are slowly yielding to the frost, and what with the odors and the tinkle and patter of the water, one might imagine himself in the court of the Alhambra, where the fountains murmur of the Moors, just as the pila of the Inca tells its inarticulate tale of a race departed, and to whose taste and poetry it bears melodious witness.

Side View of "Palace of the Inca," Island of Titicaca

The water comes through subterranean passages from sources now unknown, and never diminishes in volume. It flows today as freely as when the Incas resorted here and cut the steep hillsides into terraces, bringing the earth to fill them, so runs the legend, all the way from the Valley of Yucay, or Vale of Imperial Delights, four hundred miles distant. However that may be, this is the garden par excellence of the Collao, testifying equally to the taste, enterprise, and skill of those who created it in spite of the most rigorous of climes and most ungrateful of soils.

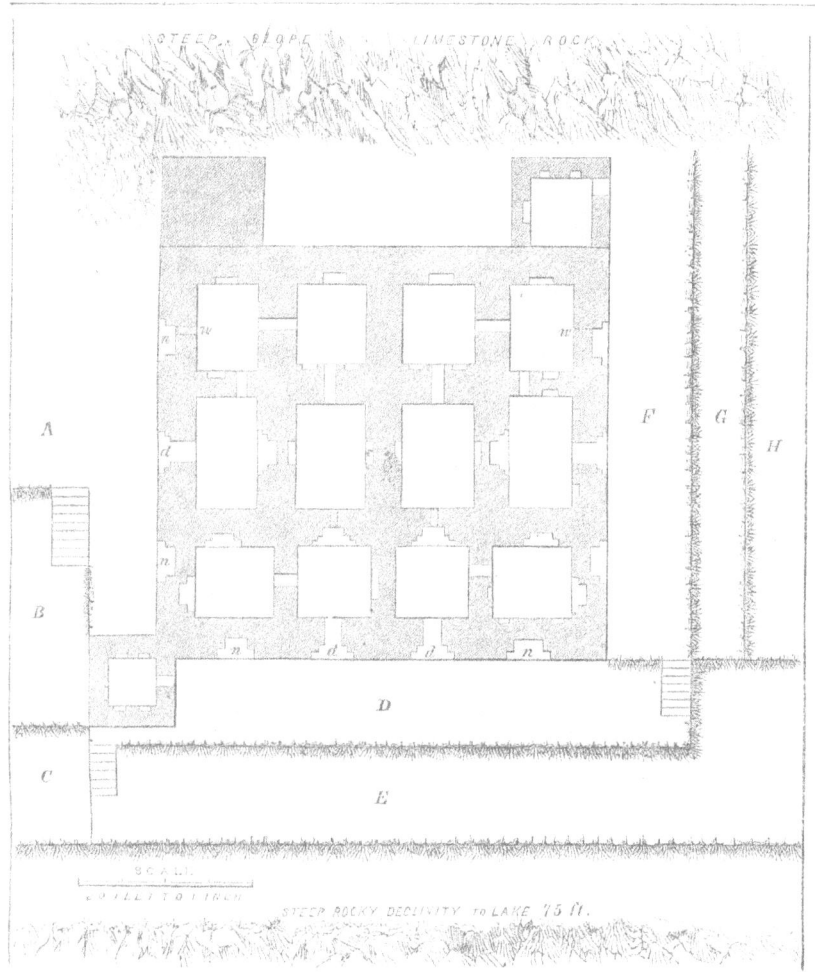

Ground Pland of "Palace of the Inca"

Half-way from the Garden of the Incas to the embarcadero, standing on a natural shelf or terrace overlooking the lake, but much smoothed by art, is El Palacio del Inca, the Palace (so called) of the Inca, to which I have already made a brief reference. Its site is beautiful. On either side are terraces, some of them niched and supporting small dependent structures, while the steep hill behind, which bends around it like a half moon, is also terraced in graceful curves, each defined not alone by its stone facing; but by a vigorous growth of the shrub that yields the Flor del Inca, which blossoms here all the year round.

The building called the Palace is rectangular, 51 by 44 feet, and two stories high.

The front on the lake is ornamented or relieved on the lower story by four high niches, the two central ones being doorways. On each side are three niches, the central one forming a doorway. It is divided into twelve small rooms, of varying sizes, and connected with each other in a manner that can only be made intelligible by reference to the plan. There are altogether four sets of rooms, two groups of two each, and two of four each. These rooms are about 13 feet high, their walls inclining slightly inward, while their ceiling is formed by flat, overlapping stones, laid with great regularity. Every room has its niches, some small and plain, others large and elaborate. The inner as well as the exterior walls were stuccoed with a fine, tenacious clay, possibly mixed with some adhesive substance, and painted. Some patches of this stucco still remain, and indicate that the building was originally yellow, while the inner parts and mouldings of the doorways and niches were of different shades of red.

Island of Coati and the "Crown of the Andes," from Esplanade of Palace of the Incas

The second story does not at all correspond in plan with the first. Its entrance is at the rear, on a level with a terrace extending back to the hill, and spreading out in a noble walk faced with a niched wall, and supporting some minor buildings or "summer houses," now greatly ruined. It appears to have had no direct connection with the ground story by stairs or otherwise. The rooms, which are also more or less ornamented with niches, are separated by walls much less massive than those below, and do not seem to have been arched as those are, but to have been roofed with thatch, as were most of the structures of the Incas. The central part of the front of the second story was not inclosed, although probably roofed, but formed an esplanade 22 feet long and 10 broad, flanked by rooms opening on it. Two niches, raised just enough to afford easy seats, appear in the wall at the back of the esplanade, whence may be commanded one of the finest and most extensive views in the world. The waves of the lake break at your very feet. To the right is the high and diversified Peninsula of Copacabana; the centre of the view, the Island of Coati, consecrated to the Moon, as was Titicaca to the Sun; and to the right the gleaming Illampu, its white mantle reflected in the waters that spread out like a sea in front. The design of this esplanade is too obvious to admit of doubt, and indicates that the builders were not deficient in taste or insensible to the grand and beautiful in nature. Tradition assigns the construction of this palace to the Inca Tupac Yupanqui, who also built the Temple of the Moon and the convent of the virgins dedicated to her service in the Island of Coati. He built it, so runs the legend, that during his visits he might always have before him the seat and shrine of the Inticoya, the sister and wife of his parent the Sun. The rooms on each side of the esplanade have each two windows, opening on the same view that I have described as to be had from the esplanade itself.

There are features, architectural and otherwise, connected with the Palace of the Inca which are of real interest, but which could only be rendered intelligible by minute plans and drawings, such as it is impossible for me to produce here. The manner in which light, or some light, was let into the lower cells or chambers, how communication was artfully established so that an order or command might be given from every point to every other point, how the terraces were sub-drained, and the water prevented from accumulating behind their stone facings, and how many other very necessary objects were accomplished—all this I must omit, and refer the inquirer to the opus that is to be, in which he will discover that the Incas and their subjects had solved very many difficult architectural and other problems, and attained very many important ends in the most rational, simple, and businesslike manner.

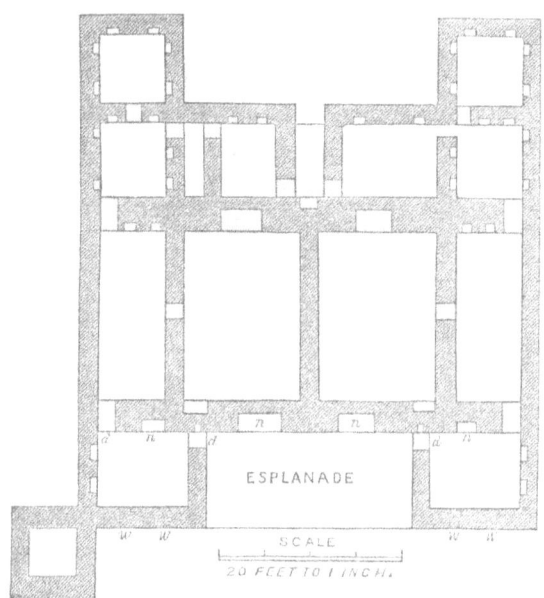

Plan of Second Story of Palace

Finding that a proper investigation of the remaining monuments of Titicaca and the other islands would require many days, and that it was tedious and difficult to get from one island to another in the clumsy balsas of the natives, I determined to push forward to Puno, the capital of the department, and make that the basis of my future operations in the Titicaca basin. Our return to the mainland was in a more pretentious and comfortable balsa than that in which we had first ventured.

Our ride back to Copacabana was a rapid one, and we found our commandante parading the streets of the town in high choler, shooting indiscriminately all dogs that he could bring his double barreled gun to bear upon. "The miserables," as he characterized the people under his care, "haven't half enough to eat themselves, and yet they will fill the town with these sneaking, snarling, starving, thieving curs. It shall not be so any longer, and I—" Here he caught sight of a dog prowling around a corner of the street; and started in pursuit. A shot and a yelp told us what had happened. The commandante soon returned, apologized for leaving us so suddenly, and conducted us to his house, saying that he knew we must be hungry.

Chambers in the "Palace of the Incas"

Our supper was scant, and the commandante, who was an able eater, rather checked his appetite, we thought, besides appearing a little abstracted and moody. The truth soon came out. Anticipating our arrival he had procured a kid in Yunguyo, and on it we were to have dined, but the famished dogs had somehow got at it, and when the time came for the cook to step in, lo! not even a bone was left. "Ni un latesito, caballeros!" said the commandante, with palpable moisture in the comers of his eyes. How many innocent dogs suffered for the sins of their fellows I know not, but they were counted by the score, and next morning not a living specimen of the genus canis was to be seen in the place. Those that survived had been carefully secreted by their owners.

The Inca's Chair

I shall not attempt here to recount the details and incidents of our journey from Copacabana to Puno. Our path was that of the traditionary Manco Capac, along the western shore of the great lake. The disrupted carboniferous strata rise in a thousand contorted and fantastic forms around us, and we see occasionally stretching away over, or rather through the hills, long trap dykes which look like titanic fortifications. We constantly encounter new and varying views, in which the lake, and its bold, brown islands, and the distant snowy Andes, are the ever recurring features. Sometimes our path lies along the sandy beach of the lake, on which the waves, driven by the fierce, cold, northeast wind, break with oceanic regularity. At intervals we reach long, straight, narrow causeways built through the shallows and marshes left by the subsidence of some ancient bay penetrating deep into the land, which were built by the Incas and have been suffered to fall into ruin by the Spaniards. Some of these are now so ruined as to be untransitable, and we find ourselves compelled to take tedious circuits along the bases of the hills to reach a spot on the other side of the morass not a thousand yards distant in a direct line. Scampering along the broken walls of inclosures, or peeping furtively out of crevices, we notice hundreds of cues or guinea pigs, indigenous to the country. Marshaled in low meadows are thousands and tens of thousands of aquatic birds, apparently in solemn conclave, which rise, if we approach too near them, with a mighty rush of wings, and a noise like that of a hail storm in a forest. At intervals of every four or five leagues we come to considerable towns, the size of which would surprise us if we did not know that in them nearly all the inhabitants of the country are gathered. Those whose occupation lies in the fields go out to their work in the morning and return at night; but during this bitter weather most of them wrap themselves in their ponchos of llama wool, and gather gloomily in their dark, filthy, unventilated cabins at night, or silently bask themselves by day on the sunny sides of their wretched habitations. Nothing more oppresses us than the stupor and gloom of the towns, which appear as if under the pall of a pestilence; and nothing repels us more than the sullen, almost morose aspect and manners of the inhabitants. A smile is seldom seen, a laugh is never heard. The impassive children never cry. It is only on the occasions of pagan festivals tolerated by the Church or incorporated with its own, and when warmed with chicha or maddened with calm, that the apathetic Aymara appears animated; it, however, is a savage, tigerish animation, which causes a shudder, but creates no sympathy.

Ancient Supulchres Acora, Peru

In these towns are great churches whose massiveness bids defiance alike to time and neglect. That of Pomata is of stone, inside and out; the very altar is cut in stone, and its roofs and walls and the niches of the saints are covered all over with a lacework of sculpture, as intricate in design as delicate in execution. The work must have been done by the Indians, before they lost the skill in stone cutting which they possessed at the time of the conquest, and to which every bolson and valley of the Sierra bears enduring witness.

Chulpas, or Burial Towers, Acora, Peru

We hear as we proceed of fortresses and other works, "muy desforme," of "El Rey Inca," but they are always far off, and we know by experience how little dependence we can put on the representations of the ignorant, who so often confound the natural with the artificial, and the trifling with the important. It is only on our third day of journeying that we find any remains of antiquity worthy of notice.

Between Juli and Illave we come upon a mass of sandstone rock, by the roadside, a hundred feet long or more, and from fifteen to twenty high. It is naturally rounded, but a stairway has been cut to its top, which is leveled artificially. Here is a seat carved in the rock, resembling a large armchair in shape and size; while lower down, in front and around, are other similar but elaborate seats, reached by other flights of steps, also cut in the rock. This, says tradition, was the "resting place of the Inca" in his journeyings or pilgrimages, where the people came to do him homage, bringing chicha for his delectation and that of his attendants.

Section of Square Chulpa

Approaching the town of Acora, three days' journey from Copacabana, we come upon a broad plain, high and arenaceous, covered with ichu grass, across which the road stretches in a long line. The plain is covered with many rude monuments, small circles and squares of unwrought upright stones planted in the ground, and sometimes sustaining others which overlap and form chambers, with openings generally toward the north. They are almost identical in appearance and character with the cromlechs of Europe, and might be transferred to Brittany or Wales, and pass for structures contemporaneous with the thousand rude monuments of antiquity found in those regions. Subsequent investigation convinced me that they were sepulchral in origin, and that they were rude and early forms of what subsequently became elaborate and symmetrical chulpas, or burial towers.

In fact, at the base of the hills bounding the plain of Acora on the west are a number of these chulpas. Some are square, others round, but all of one plan and style. Their inner mass is of rough stones laid in clay, but they are faced with hewn limestone blocks. A description of one, with the aid of a view and section, will sufficiently illustrate the character of all.

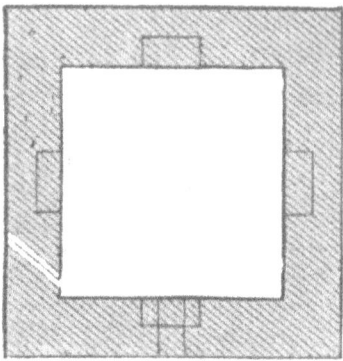

Plan of Square Chulpa

It is seventeen feet square and twenty-four feet high, and rises from a platform of cut stones twenty-two feet on each side, and raised a foot above the ground. Three feet below its top is a projection or cornice, two feet deep, projecting about a foot on every side, forming a severe but effective ornament or finish to the structure. There is a square opening, eighteen inches high and broad, in the eastern face, on a level with the platform. Crawling into this with difficulty, for it was obstructed with rubbish, I found myself in a vault, or chamber, eleven feet square and thirteen feet high, the sides of which rise vertically to the height of eight feet, where the stones begin to overlap, forming a kind of pointed arch. At the height of three feet from the floor of the vault, in the centre of each of its four faces, is a niche three feet and a half high and eighteen inches deep, with sides inclining toward each other at the top. The entrance is immediately under one of these niches. I found nothing in this dark vault except some human bones and fragments of pottery, and the gnawed bones of animals dragged here probably by dogs, for whom this had evidently been a favorite retreat.

Chulpa is the Aymara word for tomb; and near that just described is another, twenty-six feet high, and with a similar niched vault, but round instead of square. Exteriorly it has a corresponding projection or cornice, and its top is dome shaped. Its peculiar feature is that, in common with all the round chulpas, it swells outward or increases in diameter from its base to where the dome begins to spring, where it is sixteen inches more in diameter than at its foundation.

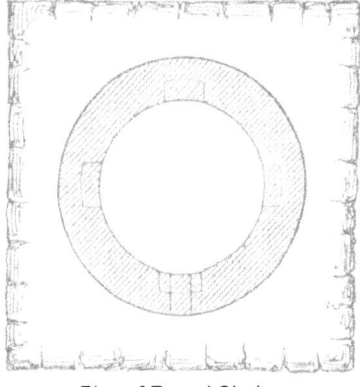

Plan of Round Chulpa

These chulpas are common in the Titicaca region, usually standing in groups of from twenty to a hundred, and almost invariably occupying some rocky ridge or spur of the hills and mountains, or some rugged eminence in the plain. Occasionally they occur singly, or in pairs. There is hardly a view to be had in the habitable districts around the head of the lake in which one or more groups do not appear, constituting a singular and interesting feature in the landscape.

Almost every traveler in the Sierra is taken for an itinerant vendor of joyas or cheap jewelry, and our instruments and iron clasped photographic boxes seemed to convey the notion that we too were vendors of paste and pinchbeck on a magnificent scale. Two leagues before reaching Puno, and just as we struck the bay on which it stands, we observed a man splendidly mounted riding rapidly toward us through the heavy sand. He drew up as we approached, removed his hat, and saluted us in grand style. We responded with equal pomp, and were speculating mentally whether he was a messenger of the Prefect of the Department or the Prefect himself, who had come to tender us the freedom and the hospitalities of the city of Puno. But he turned out to be the resident vendor of trinkets, who, hearing of our approach, had made up his mind that we were peddlers, and had come out to make us an offer for our entire stock, rather than have us open a shop and undersell him in the town. He was slow to be convinced that we were mere travelers studying the country, but when satisfied on the point gave us a contemptuous glance, and without even an adios, spurred his horse into a gallop and left us to contemplate the flutter of his receding poncho as well as we could through the dust that he raised. I do not think scientific travelers are likely to inspire profound respect or secure a very high appreciation among the mixed people of the Sierra. He must content himself to be taken for a Viracocha by the shepherd Indians.

Section of Round Chulpa

Turning sharp around a high, precipitous headland, on the shelves and among the crevices of which Indian fishermen had established their huts, looking like swallows' nests, we came in sight of Puno, standing on the shores of its bay, half grown up with totora and water plants, at the foot of the silver veined hill, or rather mountain, of Cancharani. To the famous mines of the Manto, and others, which have honeycombed the mountain, the town owes its origin. It is a large place, of between six and seven thousand inhabitants, nine-tenths of whom are pure Indians — the Aymaras occupying the southern, the Quichuas the northern portion.

We had letters to Mr. T—, an American gentleman from Philadelphia, married in the country, and the leading merchant of the place, and rode at once to his house, formerly that of General San Roman, who had been chosen President of Peru, but had just died in Lima. Here we met a hospitality such as might be expected from an ardent American who had not seen the face of a countryman for years, and here we rested a time from our journeyings.

THE CITY OF THE SUN.

Ruins of Temple of Viracocha, Cacha, Peru

I HAVE little room for Puno in this rapid narrative, but must not omit saying that it has a greater altitude than any town of its size (7000 inhabitants) in Peru or the world, except, perhaps, the mining town of Cerro de Pasco. It lacks but ten yards of being 13,000 feet above the sea. It owes its origin to the rich silver mines discovered in the mountains near it about the middle of the seventeenth century, but which, after sustaining it for a hundred and fifty years, have been practically abandoned. Wool of the sheep and alpaca, and butter, reputed the best in the world; are now its great staples of export. It is a dreary place, with low thatched houses and icy streets, through which glide noiseless llamas, and equally silent Indians, in garb sombre as that of the bare hills that circle round the town, and cut off the view in every direction except toward the lake. Here are the bright waters of the Bay of Puno, bordered all around by a broad belt of totora, and relieved by a few rocky islets, each of which has its Indian tradition, and on one of which the royalist governors confined their patriot captives during the war of the revolution, without shelter from the sun or protection from the cold.

A day or two of rest, and we began our preparations for exploring the lake and revisiting the Island of Titicaca. I have said there were no boats on Lake Titicaca. There was one, an ordinary four-oared open boat, fifteen feet long, and happily it belonged to our kind host, who introduced us to a person who had been employed in the Chilian navy, Capitan Cuadros, to whom I paid instant court. After several "surveys" of the craft, and much Bunsbyism, it was finally agreed that if her sides were raised and she were schooner-rigged, we might venture out in her on the broad and often turbulent lake. But to raise the sides —"bulwarks" Cuadros called them—was easier said than done. Where were the boards—he called the required material "timber"—to come from? The last consignment to Puno, consisting of half a dozen planks sawn in Maine, cut in sections at Islay, and brought up from the coast on mules, a twenty days' journey, had been exhausted by our host himself in making shutters for the windows of his warehouse. So we were fain to break up some goods' boxes, and build up our "bulwarks" from the pieces. The Natividad was a wonderful craft to see when all was done. Her sides were as variegated as a city dead-wall under its posters. Here you read "FRAGILE;" near by, "Tula SIDE UP, WITH CARE;" and next, "BITTERS, X. S. P. 9," in every variety of lettering. The masts were two poles which had been brought all the way from the Amazonian valleys of Carabaya, on the shoulders of Indians, and seemed to have been selected for their marvelous sinuosities. "They were too crooked," H— protested, "to lie still." A box that had been lined with tin to hold calicoes, containing a little clay furnace, was firmly fastened in the bow as a kitchen, and, by great good luck, we obtained a bag of charcoal. Captain Cuadros had a little place fenced off for him in the stern, where he acted as captain, mate, and steersman. We occupied the centre of the craft, while the two bogadores, or rowers, and Ignacio my servant, a consummate rascal, who acted as cook, went "before the mast."

In this frail vessel we navigated the lake from end to end, visited its islands and the Bolivian shores, whither we were driven in a blinding storm of snow and sleet, lasting twenty-four hours, during which nothing but assiduous bailing kept the Natividad afloat. Becalmed in returning for five days, we exhausted our stores, and for two days were without food of any kind. This is not the place to recount our adventures or discoveries. I hope the latter may ultimately be of some use to the world, for I certainly shall undertake to make no more in an open boat, on a stormy lake, two miles up in the air, with the thermometer perversely inclined to zero.

Our friends in Puno had become greatly concerned on account of our long absence; in fact, they had given us up; and when we were discerned working across the bay they hastened down to the little mole and received us with a cordial welcome, as well as with some welcome cordial.

Before leaving on our expedition I had "assisted" at a grand "function," a patriotic Festival of Flags, I should call it, symbolical of a union of all the republics against monarchical intervention in America. France was then in Mexico; Spain in Santo Domingo; and, believing that the United States was in the throes of dissolution, the buzzards of reaction were hovering on the coasts of the Pacific, ready to swoop down on the rich but petty republics that lie there, and reduce them again to a state of colonial dependence. I had signed an "acto" on the occasion; and what was more, had carried an American flag, which the young ladies of the Colejio had improvised for the occasion, getting the number of the stripes wrong, and the azure field a world too little, but making up for all in the size and weight of the staff—one of the poles, I verily believe, that afterward answered for a mast in the Natividad. But that was not the worst. We had to go through a mass and a benediction of the banderas in the chill cathedral, with many genuflexions and much kneeling on the cold stones, besides enduring a speech from the prefect afterward, with heads uncovered, in the frosty air. The American flag had been given the post of honor, with those of Chili and Mexico on either hand. And as by a remarkable and unprecedented coincidence two young American engineers had arrived in Puno, so that the Yankee element mustered four strong, and in part recognition of the high honor given to the United States on the occasion of the function, Mr. T— determined that the Glorious Fourth, then close at hand, should be celebrated by a dinner, and "with all the honors."

And it was so celebrated. The brass six-pounder of the place was fired, a gun for each State, at sunrise; the bells were pealed at noon; a mass for the good deliverance of the United States was performed in the cathedral at two o'clock; the garrison was paraded as an escort to the American flag, which was carried in triumph through the streets; and, altogether, Puno held high holiday on the 4th of July, 1864. Even the morose Aymaras seemed to relent, and a few of the more volatile Quichuas were seen to smile. It was the grand fiesta of St. Jonathan, and chicha could be had gratis in the plaza.

A severe hurt received through a fall among the ruins of Coati, and a fever superinduced by exposure on the lake, kept me from taking an active part in the entertainment and ball that followed the festivities of the day, which were shared in cordially, and with genuine sympathy, by all the people of Puno who had ever heard of the United States—the most respectable, but by no means the most numerous class. I regretted this, as it prevented me from witnessing an incident which I can not help relating, and which, while it illustrates some things in Peru, is not to be taken as characteristic of the people.

It must be premised that in the smaller towns of Spanish America the plebe invite themselves to witness, if not exactly to participate in, any tertulia or social gathering that may take place. The style of buildings, around a court entered by a zaguan or single great doorway, precludes much exclusiveness, even if attempted. The court of Mr. T—'s house was consequently filled, not alone while dinner was going on, but afterward; and policy, as well as regard for custom, would have induced him to be extremely liberal of solids as well as liquids to the "outsiders." Most of these left when the invited and presumably more respectable guests departed; but a few inveterates, who had got a taste of genuine cognac, persisted in remaining in hope of another trago. The great door was closed at midnight and merely the wicket left open—a hint to leave which only two or three of the self-invited guests or spectators failed to understand. Finally all had departed except a stalwart mestizo, who wore a long and ample cloak—everybody needs to wear a cloak in the Sierra—who lingered and chatted, and chatted and lingered, until Mr. T—, imagining that all he wanted was brandy, gave him half a bottle, and, gently crowding him toward the wicket, said, "Now, my friend, it is past two o'clock, I am very tired, and really you must go!"

"Open the door," responded the man with the cloak.

"Surely you can go out by the wicket. Why should I open the door?"

"To let me out."

This was too much, and our host, in a fit of irritation, gave the persistent intruder a push. Staggering, he dropped a ladies' parlor chair that he had concealed under his cloak, darted through the wicket, and disappeared in the darkness.

Besides our long excursion on the lake we made several expeditions to places of interest around Puno. One of these was to the remarkable lake of Umayo, six leagues to the northeast of Puno, and four from Lake Titicaca. It lies at a higher level than the latter, is about twelve miles in circuit, surrounded on nearly all sides by abrupt cliffs 300 feet high, and might be taken for a vast, ancient crater, except for a large island in its centre, with its summit level with the plain in which the lake is sunk. The town of Vilque stands near one extremity of the lake, and is celebrated for its annual fair, which is attended by people from a thousand miles' distance—from Cuzco on the north to Tucuman and the provinces of the La Plata on the southeast. Droves of mules are brought from this direction for the supply of the Sierra, where the raising of sheep is more profitable than that of beasts of burden. Beyond Vilque lying high up among the Cordillera, are other considerable lakes, one of which, called Coallaqui, is not far from 17,000 feet above the sea.

The lake of Umayo, although represented on the maps as discharging into Lake Titicaca, has really no outlet. It nevertheless contains several varieties of fishes, some of which, if not all, are identical with those of the greater lake. It was on the shores of Umayo that the powerful chiefs of the Collao, before their reduction by the Incas, had their capital, Hatun-Colla; and the headlands of the lake and the heights around it bristle with their burial towers or chulpas. These are generally of rough stones cemented together by a tenacious clay; but on the bold peninsula of Sillustani is a group of the largest and best built of all these structures to be found in Peru.

Most of the towers are round, swelling upward, as I have already described, and terminating in perfectly symmetrical domes. Blocks of stone from eight to twelve feet long and from five to six feet thick are built in some of these, and keyed in place with admirable skill. All are vaulted, and some have two tiers of niches for receiving the dead. On the isthmus, connecting the peninsula with the mainland, the Incas had built an edifice, probably religious, now in ruins, but retaining the name of Inti-cancha inclosure or house of the Sun.

There are, however, on the peninsula other remains which, like the cromlechs of Acora, have a special interest from their absolute identity with the very earliest monuments of mankind, and which are indistinguishable from what in Northern Europe and the British Islands are called Sun or Druidical circles. They are here called Inti-huatana, literally "place where the Sun is tied up."

Sun Circle, Sillustani, Peru

Some of these circles are more elaborate than others, and of one of these I give a drawing that will serve to illustrate all. It will be observed that there is first a circle of rough, upright stones, of irregular sizes, firmly set in the ground. The circle is 124 feet in diameter; it has an opening 5 feet wide on the east, and it incloses two larger upright stones (one of which has fallen), placed one-third of the diameter of the circle apart.

Outside of the circle thus formed is a cincture of broad, flat stones, roughly shaped by art, which lie flat on the ground and form a kind of platform four feet and a half broad. The adjoining edges of these stones are on radii from the centre of the circle. Their inner ends, or the parts nearest the upright stones and adjoining them, are raised, forming a kind of beading running entirely around the circle. In this is cut a channel or groove, three inches deep and four and a half inches wide, which also extends entirely around the circle. The stones at the sides of the entrance or gateway are pierced with holes, as shown in the engraving, as if for the reception of ropes.

Platform Stone of Sun Circle

This is the perfected form of the sun-circles of Peru, and it must not be supposed that all of them are equally elaborate, for the greater number are composed of simple upright stones in their natural state.

A few instances have fallen under my notice in the vast region that composed the Inca Empire, in which rough upright stones, often of large size, were arranged in the form of squares or rectangles. The celebrated ruins of Tiahuanaco, in Bolivia, described in a previous article, afford a most striking example. Here we find quadrangles defined by great unhewn stones, worn and frayed by time, and having every evidence of the highest antiquity, side by side with other squares of similar plan, but defined by massive stones cut with much elaboration, as if they were the works or later and more advanced generations, which, however, still preserved the motions of their ancestors, bringing only greater skill to the construction of their monuments.

132

I shall not advance any hypothesis concerning the massive remains of Tiahuanaco, but content myself by observing what every student of antiquity will recognize as true, that the square was often associated with the circle in solar symbolism, and in that worship which seems to have been, throughout the world, the earliest adopted by its inhabitants. Striking and numerous illustrations of this may be found in the vast earthen structures scattered over the United States, and which seem to have an antiquity that few are bold enough to affirm, but which must be measured if not by geological, by semi-geological epochs.

The bay, that sweeps behind the peninsula of Sillustani is shallow, grown up with reeds, and with the lake weed which I have described as affording food for cattle in the dry season, and which is called Ilachu. A part of the area now covered by the bay, tradition affirms, was the site of the capital of the chiefs of Hatun-Colla; and certain it is that walls as if of buildings may be discerned, beneath the water, and here and there projecting above it. The little Indian village that now bears the name of Hatun-Colla, or Atun-Colla, is more than a league distant, and contains no remains of antiquity except two great jambs or square columns of stone standing in front of the house of the cura. These are sculptured on their faces, with geometrical figures, interspersed with figures of frogs, serpents, and lizards. They are said to have stood on the banks of the lake in former days.

Our journey from Puno was continued around the upper end of Lake Titicaca, through the towns of Paucarcolla, Pusi, and Taraco, to Huancané, near the head of the fine bay of that name, crossing the considerable rivers Lampa and Ramis, not far above their mouths. Both these streams are erroneously laid down in the maps. The former does not flow direct into the lake, but into the bay of Puno.

Between Paucarcolla and Pusi we stopped to explore certain monuments that we discovered wide of our road, and sent our baggage ahead. Night came on without our overtaking it, and becoming entangled among the hills of Capachica we lost the trail, and were obliged to pass the cold night by the side of a rock, without food or fire, or any covering except our ponchos. When day dawned we found ourselves less than half a league from the town to which we were bound, where, in the firm belief that we had been drowned in crossing the Lampa River, Ignacio had commenced administering on our effects, and, with the arrieros, at half an hour after daylight, was "drunk as a lord" on our best cognac. Drunkenness is universal throughout the Sierra. Nothing that can be made to ferment is neglected in manufacturing intoxicating beverages. Nearly all the maize is converted into dacha; even the berries of the trees. And as for the cane that is grown in the hot valleys, its juice is wholly distilled into cañaso, so that sugar in Cuzco can only be had at from a dollar to a dollar and a half a pound!

Turf House Near Mouth of Rio Ramos

The region around the mouth of the Ramos is a kind of delta, very low and level, interspersed with shallow pools, as if but recently half rescued from the lake by deposits from the river. These pools are thronged with water-fowl, among which the scarlet ibis and strong-winged mountain goose are conspicuous. The inhabitants here are all shepherds; and as what there is of solid ground is covered with a thin but tough turf, this is used exclusively in constructing their dwellings and the pens or corrales for their flocks. Quaint and curious structures they are, looking like tall, quadrilateral haystacks. In some attempts had been made at something like architectural adornment, and, like the chulpas, these have a kind of cornice at the point where the roof begins to converge from the vertical walls—a feature suggested perhaps by the chulpas, or a tradition of style descending from the ancient builders of the tombs. In their interior they are, in common with all the dwellings of the Indian natives, filthy in the extreme. A few had been deserted and fallen down, forming mounds of more or less regularity and elevation, in which excavation would certainly expose what we generally find in mounds of earth all over the world—bones, fragments of pottery, some battered implements not worth removal, and traces of fire.

The town of Huancané is large, and occupied almost exclusively by Indians of Aymara family. It has some hot springs in its neighborhood, which have a high medicinal reputation, and the place may be regarded as the Saratoga of the Puno district. Four leagues beyond, following the shores of the bay of Huancané, is the Indian pueblo of Vilquechico, in the neighborhood of which are other hot springs, the Inca ruins of Acarpa, and the Pre-Incarial monuments of Quellenata, which I have not space to describe here. They consist of a vast number of chulpas, of various sizes, standing on an eminence that may justly be called a mountain, surrounded by walls of rough or rudely-fashioned stones, pierced with doorways, indistinguishable from what in the Old World are called Pelasgic walls. The ruins of Acarpa stand on a peninsula projecting far into a shallow bay, and were reached by the Incas over causeways of stone still visible above the water.

Leaving Huancané, where since our visit the Indians have risen in open revolt against the whites and committed great cruelties, we traveled northwest through the town of Chupe to Azangaro, one of the most famous seats of the ancient inhabitants, and distinguished now as containing one of the most remarkable monuments of antiquity in Peru, the Sondor-huasi or Roundhouse, which retains its original thatched roof after a lapse of over three hundred years, showing us how much of skill and beauty as well as utility may be achieved and displayed, even in a roof of thatch. We know, from the concurrent testimony of the chroniclers, that all the Inca roofs were of thatch —as indeed nine-tenths of the roofs of all of the buildings of the Sierra still are. From this has been inferred an incongruity between the skillful workmanship of the walls and the rude character and meanness of the roofs, which the Sondor-huasi will go far to correct. The thin, long, and tough ichu grass of this mountain region is admirably adapted for thatch, lying smoothly, besides being readily worked.

The dome of the Sondor-huasi is perfect, and is formed of a series of bamboos of equal size and taper, their larger ends resting on the top of the walls—bent evenly to a central point, over a series of hoops of the same material and of graduated sizes. At the points where the vertical and horizontal supports cross each other they are bound together by fine cords of delicately-braided grass, which cross and re-cross each other with admirable skill and taste. Over this skeleton dome is a fine mat of the braided epidermis of the bamboo or rattan, which, as it exposes no seams, almost induces the belief that it was braided on the spot. However that may be, it was worked in different colors and in panelings conforming in size with the diminishing spaces between the framework, that framework itself being also painted. I shall probably shock my classical readers and be accounted presumptuous when I venture a comparison of the Azangaro dome, in style and effect, with that of the Pella of the temple of Venus and Rome, facing the Coliseuni in the Eternal City.

Over this inner matting is another, open, coarse, and strong, in which was fastened a fleece of finest ichu, which depends like a heavy fringe outside the walls. Next comes a transverse layer of coarser grass or reeds, to which succeeds ichu, and so on, the whole rising in the centre so as to form a slightly flattened cone. The projecting ends of the ichu layers were cut off sharply and regularly, producing the effect of overlapping tiles.

From Azangaro our route lay over a high tableland covered with snow, into the Valley of the Rio Pucura, which we ascended through the towns of Pucura and Ayavira to Santa Rosa, a considerable town, the last of the Collao, at the foot of the great snowy mountain of Apucumurami.

Here we witnessed one of those bullfights, or rather bull baitings, which are the delight equally of the people of the coast and the Sierra. The plaza of the town was fenced in, and the bull, with a gaudy crimson cloth fastened over his back, and his horns loaded with firecrackers, was let into the inclosure. Then commenced the process of tormenting the animal. To mount on the bull's back and ride him round the plaza, while lighting the fireworks; to prod him with sharp nails set in the ends of poles, and generally to irritate and vex him, while dextrously escaping his blind wrath, seems to constitute this cherished pastime.

At Santa Rosa the performances were varied by fastening a young condor on the back of one of the bulls, which when roused by the noise, the motion, and the explosions began to beat the sides of the bull with his powerful wings, and to lacerate his flesh with his terrible beak. After both bull and condor had become completely exhausted, and the former with bleeding flanks and protruding tongue was standing helplessly in a corner, an Indian approached to unfasten the bird, which, however, seized him by the arm and nearly tore it from its socket. This condor with another was given me by their owner; and I undertook to send them home as a present to the Central Park. They, however, never reached the coast, as the following letter from Pedro Lobo, the arriero, who undertook to take them there, will, perhaps, sufficiently explain:

"Sir and Gentleman, Viracocha!

"I am ill. I supplicate your mercy. I am a poor man, as you know, and my family has had the smallpox. Manuela died, it is now a long time. There is little alfalfa to be had in my village. So I ask your forgiveness. I could not do otherwise. It happened so. It was in the Pampa of Tungasaca. One of the pollos (chickens), he of the bull, tore off the ears of the mule Chepa who carried him. You remember the mule Chepa, because of its tail, which was short. It made strings of my poncho, and grievously hurt me. I still crave your mercy. But it got away.

"You know that maize is very high, and, as I said before, poor Manuela died of the smallpox. They are taking men for the army. I don't know what may happen to me. There is measles in my village, and the roads are bad; but when the pollo of the torn got away, the other got away also. I know they will say in Santa Rosa that I cut the straps. And so it may appear. But Sir, Gentleman, and Viracocha, you will not believe them; for there is little alfalfa and no maize to mention in my village; and it is now two years since Manuela died, to say nothing of the measles, from which may the Virgin protect your worship. I Hence I ask your mercy."

I should explain that I had on several occasions expressed great sympathy with Pedro Lobo on account of the premature death of his daughter Manuela, and he argued that the reference would soften my heart and avert any anger I might experience on account of the escape of the pollos.

At Santa Rosa the Andes and Cordillera are knotted together, and we soon become involved among their gorges, disputing passageway with the headwaters of the river of Pucura. From Santa Rosa to the divide, a weary distance of five leagues, the scenery is most bold and impressive, resembling that of the valley of the Lauterbrunnen, in Switzerland, or the ascent of the pass of St. Gothard from Bellemzona. There are no habitations, only here and there, at exposed points, remains of Inca tambos, under whose crumbling walls we find some shivering groups of native travelers, huddled together over a smouldering fire of dung, endeavoring to warm their wretched chupe. The wind forces itself through the gorges with fearful force, driving before it the sand and gravel of the rough pathway and fine splinters of disintegrating rock, which puncture the chapped and smarting skin like lancets, until the blood starts in drops from every exposed part of the person. Our mules rebel against facing the blast, and obstinately turn their backs toward it, or viciously refuse to leave the shelter of some rock that breaks the force of the wind. The mountains all around us are covered with snow, which occasionally drives down in blinding whirls upon us, when some avalanche breaks away from the impending crests that curve over like the combing waves of the ocean before they break on the shore. We approach a narrow pass; a frosty stream, curdled with floating snow and icy crystals, frets between the rough rocks on one side, and the cliff rises sheer on the other, with only a narrow shelf for the roadway, so narrow that the animals can not pass abreast. We have just entered on it, with a hurt cargo mule now running de valde, or free, ahead, when we hear the sound of the warning whistle of some party approaching us from the other end of the pass, and which we had heard before, but half deaf and blinded, had confounded it with the shriek of the cruel wind. We make an attempt to turn back the mule, but she plunges forward, while we retreat to a wider part of the shelf and flatten ourselves against the rock to permit the approaching travelers to pass. They prove to be a man evidently of position, but wearing a thick mask and goggles, who answers to our inquiry if he had encountered a mule, by pointing down among the rocks at the foot of the precipice. He had shot the animal as it confronted him in the road; there was no other alternative.

As we approach the summit the gorge widens out a little, and we have a better road. Here we find every rock supporting heaps of stones, and there are hundreds of other heaps on all sides where there is room enough to build them up, from a foot to five and more feet high. They have been raised by the Indians in propitiation to the spirits of the mountains, and those which control the winds and the snows and the bitter frosts. The river of Pucura, reduced in size to a mere brook, babbles at our side, and we feel as grateful as the Indians themselves, albeit we do not rear our little apachita in token of having passed safely the worst part of our road. A mile further, and we reach the cumbre or divide—a lap, if I may, use the term, between the two mountain ranges. Here, on one side, is a great apachita or pile of votive stones, and on the other a small lake or tarn, welling up among masses of vibrating, half-frozen turf, edged round with a silvery border of ice, and looking clear but dark under the cold, steel-like sky.

From this lake, which is only a few hundred feet across, flow two small, distinct streams—one through the gorge we have passed southward, forming in its course the River Pucura, falling into Lake Titicaca, and the other flowing north, constituting the source of the Rio Vilcanota, which, under its successive names of Vilcamayo, Yucay, Urubamba, and Ucayali, forms the true parent stream of the Amazon. A cork thrown into the centre of the lake might be carried into Titicaca or into the Atlantic, depending probably on the direction of the wind.

The divide which we have reached is in latitude 14° 30' S., and longitude 70° 50' W., at an elevation of 14,500 feet, dominated by the great snowy peak of Vilcanota, which still rises majestically above us.

Around the lake are the remains of several Inca tambos, some evidently designed for the poorer order of travelers, and one clearly intended for the Inca himself, or those of his blood. The latter has been most destroyed by the seekers for treasure, and its leveled walls afford no protection from the winds. So we gather for the night under the lee of some standing walls of humbler structures, fasten our mules close beside us, feeding them with raw barley, and, fencing ourselves in with our baggage, huddle around a little fire of sticks of quinua, which, by a fortunate accident, we were able to buy in Santa Rosa at a little less than their weight in silver. We refresh ourselves with coffee; our arrieros stuff their mouths with coca; we pack ourselves together as closely as possible, and await the dawn, when we shall start down the slopes of the Amazon.

The means of intercommunication in the Inca Empire, under the beneficent rule of its aboriginal sovereigns, were infinitely better than they are today. Apart from their roads and bridges, they built at all exposed points, at intervals in the puns and among the mountains, as well as in the villages, posts or tambos for the accommodation of travelers. These were by no means imposing, but large and comfortable, structures, in which not alone the travelers themselves but their llamas might find food and shelter. At La Raya, through which all communication between the capital and the Colla-suya, or important region around Lake Titicaca, had to pass, the public requirements were met by the construction of a number of tambos of large size; and there are also traces of a fortification, as if for the maintenance here of a garrison. I made a plan of one of these tambos, under the crumbling walls of which we found protection for the night, which may be taken as a type of this kind of structures in general, although no two are precisely alike. It is a building with a front of 180 feet in length, with wings extending inward at either. extremity, forming three sides of a court. This court is extended down to the waters of the little lake by rough stone-walls, and the ground falls off by low terraces. The main front has but three rooms, each about sixty feet long; the central one alone having entrances from the outside. The corner rooms open into the court, and each has a smaller inner room that can only be reached through it—designed, perhaps, for the women or persons of distinction. The rooms have small niches on their sides, sunk in the walls, which are from two to three feet thick, composed of rough stones laid in clay. Altogether, the tambos seem to have been rough but substantial, common sense structures, rationally devised to meet the wants of the people for whose use they were built. The courts were no doubt designed for the reception of the herds or llamas and alpacas that might accompany travelers, or be sent from the valleys to the plains of the Collao.

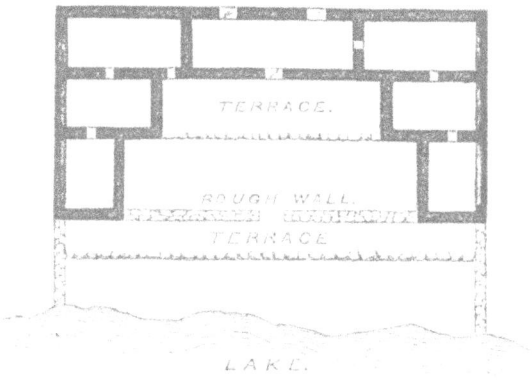

Plan of Inca Tambo, La Raya

Descending now, here between steep mountains where stream and roadway dispute the passage, with eternal winter enthroned on the heights above us, anon urging our mules over narrow but arable intervals of land, or stopping to rest in quaint villages of Indians, famous in aboriginal history as the Canchas, we prosecute our journey sixty miles further, until the stream that trickled from the tarn of La Raya has swollen to be an unfordable river, under the name of Vilcanota. Here we reach the town of Cacha, near which are the remains of the famous temple of Viracocha. The valley has spread out to the width of a league, and is level and fertile. Beyond the town, on the right bank of the river, and rising nearly in the centre of the valley, is the broad and rather low volcanic cone of Haratche. It has thrown out its masses of lava on all sides, partly filling up the hollow between it and the mountains on one hand, and sending off two high dykes to the river on the other. Between these dykes is a triangular space, nearly a mile in greatest length, literally walled in by ridges of black lava, heaped in wildest confusion to the height of many feet. At the upper end of this space, which has been widened by terracing up against the lava fields, and piling back the rough fragments on each other, is a copious spring, sending out a considerable stream. It has been carefully walled in with cut stones, and surrounded with terraces, over the edges of which it falls, in musical cataracts, into a large artificial pond or reservoir covering several acres of area, in which grow aquatic plants, and in which water birds find congenial refuge. From this pond the water discharges itself, partly through numerous azequias that irrigate the various terraces lining this lava bound valley, and partly through a walled channel into the Vilcanota.

Overlooking the reservoir or pond, on a broad terrace or rather series of terraces, in the middle of a great semicircular area, rise the lofty remains of the Temple of Viracocha, one of the most important ever raised by the Incas, and which seems to have been entirely unique in character. It is surrounded by remains of other structures of regular design, covering a wide space. The most conspicuous part of the remains is a high wall of adobes, rising on a base of worked stone to the height of upward of sixty feet, and showing evidences of having been part of a building three stories in height. One or two tall columns, built in like manner, still remain, and one gable of the building. The dependent structures are those of edifices raised round a succession of quadrangular courts on terraces, and fenced off by high walls from a grand series of square and circular buildings of inferior design and workmanship. A view of the central walls of this temple is given at the head of this article.

I can not stop to give a particular account of this wonderful building, nor have I space to repeat the traditions connected with its origin. I must content myself by saying that I regard the structure as second to none in Peru in interest, architecturally or otherwise.

I can not, however, refrain from correcting one or two radical errors that have obtained as regards Inca architecture, and which have received the support of the great names of Humboldt and Prescott. The former, in his account of the fortress of Cannar, in the northern part of the Inca Empire, describes a building within its walls which, though smaller, was nearly a counterpart of the double houses found near the Temple of Viracocha. He seems to have been surprised to find that the edifice had gables like those of our own dwellings, and expresses his belief that they were added after the conquest. The fact of the existence of windows in these gables he regarded as specially favoring that hypothesis; "for it is certain," he adds, "that in the edifices of Peruvian construction as in the remains of the houses of Pompeii and Herculaneum, no windows are to be found." M. de la Condamine before him had expressed some doubts of the antiquity of the gables, but thought it possible that they formed a part of the ancient structure. Prescott, probably following Humboldt, denies the existence of windows in Peruvian architecture.

Humboldt, however, saw but few Inca remains in Northern Peru. Had he journeyed in the centre or southern parts of the country he would have found the use of gables and of windows almost universal. Gables are even to be found among the ruins of Grand Chimu on the coast, where rain seldom falls. Everywhere in the interior the ruins of Inca towns are specially marked by their pointed gables, which have almost always one and frequently two windows. These windows were sometimes used as doorways for entrance to the upper or half story of the edifice, and were reached by a succession of flat stones projecting from the walls so as to form a flight of steps.

It was on the heights of Tungasaca overlooking the ruins of the Temple of Viracocha, on the opposite bank of the river, that José Gabriel Condorcanqui, better known by the name be ultimately assumed of Tupac-Amaru, organized, toward the close of the last century, that uprising of the Indians against the Spaniards which soon spread throughout the Sierra, and threatened the extinction of the Spanish power in Peru. Tupac-Amaru was the lineal descendant of the last of the Incas, and when he gathered his followers in the town of Tinta, on his way to wrest the capital of his fathers from the hands of the descendants of Pizarro, he led them first to the ruins of the Temple of Viracocha, and there, surrounded by black and rugged lava walls, and under the shadow of the crumbling sanctuary, with strange and solemn ceremonies and ancient invocations, adjured the aid of the Spirit that fought by the side of the young Viracocha on the plain of Yauhaur Pampa. For a time he was successful; the dead gods seemed to live once more, and the banner of the Incas, glowing anew with its iris blazon, seemed destined to float again above the massive walls of the great fortress of Cuzco. But treachery more than force ruined the cause of the Indian chieftain; he was taken prisoner, and, after being obliged to witness the execution of his wife and son, was himself, May 21, 1781, torn in pieces by horses in the great square of Cuzco, and under the walls of its august cathedral, dedicated to the service of a just and merciful God.

Gateway of Fortress of Piquillacta

After leaving Cacha we find nothing of special interest until we reach a point where the mountains close in on both sides of the Vilcanota and leave it only a rock-bound cañon wherein to flow. Here we leave the valley and ascending an abrupt ridge to the left enter the village of Urcos, beyond which, in a deep depression of the land, lies the little yellow lake of Urcos, with neither inlet nor outlet, and in which the great golden chain of Huayna Capac is said to have been thrown to save it from the avarice of the Spaniards—a chain that "reached twice around the great square of Cuzco." The drift undertaken in Garcilosso's time, and driven for a hundred yards in the solid rock, for the purpose of draining the lake and recovering the hidden treasure, is still visible.

From the Calvario beyond Urcos we get our first view of the rich and beautiful valley of Andahuaylillas, one of those valleys, lying laterally to the great watercourses of the country, and considerably elevated above them, which form a distinctive feature of this portion of Peru, and in one of which Cuzco is situated. These valleys vary from five to fifteen miles in length, by half as much in width, and lie intermediately as regards elevation between the high, cold, arid table lands or puns, where cultivation is impossible, and the deep, narrow, and often fervid channels of the great rivers. They are always well watered, collecting the sills that descend from the hills on every hand into a single bright and often considerable stream, Which breaks through some deep, dark, rocky gorge, and by a series of brawling rapids and foaming cataracts discharge themselves into the great tributaries of the Amazon.

We will not linger in the beautiful little valley of Andahuaylillas, excepting for a moment near its northern extremity, where, approaching the hills again, we see a vast area covered with broken stones piled up in great heaps, while all around are blocks of fine grained trachyte, squared with the highest precision of the stonecutter, and looking as if but yesterday turned out from under his dextrous chisel. We will not require to be told by our arriero that this is one of the old Inca quarries; for the rude stone buildings in which the quarrymen lived cluster all over the hillsides, and even in their ruin betray the unmistakable characteristics of Inca architecture. We shall find, when we get to Cuzco, now distant twenty miles, that the stones for the Temple of the Sun and the royal palaces were taken from these quarries, which cover an area hardly less than a mile square.

A mile or so beyond the quarries, the valley still contracting and our path ascending, we come to the Pass of Piquillacta, hemmed in by cliffs, within a width of 2000 feet. Here, rising before us, we find a massive wall of stones, between twenty and thirty feet in height, pierced by two gateways—a wall more massive than that which surrounded Latinum. The gateways are faced with stones cut with skill and laid, albeit without cement, with such precision that we can scarcely insert the thinnest knife-blade between them. This is the Fortress of Piquillacta, which was the southern limit of the dominions of the first Inca—whose steps we have followed from the island of Titicaca. Inside the wall are the remains of the guard-houses or barracks wherein dwelt the defenders of his narrow domain against the Canchas, Who were brought under Inca rule by his successor. A well graded road leads hence to a vast group of ruins of the extensive ancient walled town of Nunn, laid out with avenues and streets and public squares. The lake of Oropesa lies to our left, and the village of the same name at our feet, while the white, Moorish-looking buildings of numerous haciendas glisten in the sun, at intervals, along the base of the hills on every hand. We press by them all, scarcely heeding their beauties, for we know the Inca capital is close before us, and we must reach it ere nightfall. The valley contracts; again the passage is disputed by stream and roadway. We are in the Pass of Angostura—the Narrows. A few hundred yards more, the heights all around us crowned with the tall gables of ruined Inca structures, we reach a point where the valley of Cuzco opens on our sight. An oblong valley shut in by treeless mountains, the air shimmering with the seemingly palpable golden bars of the declining sun, underneath which, past the clustering villages of San Sebastian and San Geronimo, at the head and most elevated part of the valley, reclining in calm repose of shadow against the amber colored hills, the slant light gleaming on the tops of its threescore towers, whence the low vibration of bells, in whose solid masses are melted the gold and silver idols of an ancient Faith, reach our expectant ears—here we pause, and in sympathetic action with our muleteers, who remove their hats and bow their heads low to the earth, we too salute reverently the City of the Sun!

We pass through the village of San Sebastian, where the haughtiness of the people might tell us, if we knew it not before, that they are the descendants of the ayllos, lineages or families of Inca blood, who, after the conquest, were assigned this spot as a refuge; and, striking a paved road, we hurry on toward the city of our destination. We enter it at the plaza of Rimac Pampa (the plain of the oracle), and, between buildings raised on massive, ancient foundations, adobes on stone—modern on ancient art—the gutter occupying the middle of the street, and by no means redolent of the odors of Araby the Blest, we slowly reach the Inti-pampa, or Square of the Sun, where the serpent-covered walls on every side betray their Inca origin.

Here we inquire for the principal plaza, and are directed through a narrow street, darkened by heavy walls of stones cut with marvelous precision, impressive in their originality, pierced here and there with doorways, narrowing at the top, which bring back recollections of Egypt; and by-and-by we emerge in a great square with a central fountain, the Huaca-pata, or Sacred Terrace of the Incas, now flanked by a heavy cathedral on one side, the elaborate church of the Jesuits on another, and surrounded by a low colonnade. It is night, and when we inquire for the residence of the commandante of the forces—there are no hotels in Cuzco—a showily-dressed officer undertakes to conduct us thither, points to a heavy archway, beneath which our weary animals, conscious of a refuge at last, dash with unwonted and startling vigor, and we find ourselves the welcome guests of Colonel Francisco Vargas, whose name, it is only due, I shall ever mention with respect and gratitude—a respect and gratitude which all my readers would share had they undergone the privations, the hunger and thirst, the cold, exposure, and annoyances that were really involved in the long and weary journey, of which I have written so lightly, from the distant coast to this lofty eyrie of aboriginal power.

We are finally in Cuzco, where Manco Capac's magic wand sank into the earth, and where he commenced the fulfillment of the high and beneficent mission intrusted to him by his father the Sun. Here he built his palace, here his successors founded theirs, and here in due time arose that splendid fane, the Temple of the Sun, with the palaces of its ministers and the convents of its vestals. Above it frowns the great fortress of Sacsahuaman, the work of three reigns, the most massive and enduring monument of aboriginal art on the American continent, and which the wondering chroniclers pronounced to be the ninth great wonder of the world. *["Cuzco," wrote Colonel, afterward Marshal, O'Leary to General Miller, during the war of Peruvian Independence, "interests me greatly. Its history, its fables, its ruins are enchanting. It may with truth be called the Rome of the New World. The immense fortress on the north is the Capitol. The Temple of the Sun is its Coliseum. Manco Capac was its Romulus; Viracocha its Augustus; Huascar its Pompey, and Atahnalpa its Caesar. The Pizarros, Almagros, Valdivias, and Toledos are the Finns, Goths, and Christians who destroyed it. Tupac Amara is its Belisarius who gave it a day of hope. Pumacagua its Rienzi and last patriot."]*

Before, however, going into a description of the city and its objects of interest, let us pause it moment to notice its position, its climate, and the favorable conditions which contributed to make it the seat of empire. Its very name, Cuzco, which signifies the umbilicus or navel, was not given to it after the Inca dominion had been widely extended by warlike princes, but at the very period of its foundation, to denote that its position was central and dominating. The bolson or pocket in which it is situated is the central one of a group or cluster of such valleys, separated from each other by comparatively low passes between the mountains or hills, and is the one most easily defensible. To the north is the valley of Anta or Xaxiguana, where the Pizarros and Almagros decided the rule of Peru, and to the south is that of Andahuaylillas. The rule of the first Inca does not appear to have extended at first beyond this valley of Cuzco. The city stands at the northern or most elevated end of the valley, on the lower slopes of three high hills, where as many rivulets coming together, like the fingers of an outspread hand, unite to form the Cachimayo, the stream that disputes passage with the narrow roadway, in the Pass of Angostura. These three streams are named respectively the Rodadero or Tiillamayo, the Huatenay, and Almodena, and within and around the triangles formed by their confluence the city of Cuzco is built. The old city, or that part of it dedicated to the royal family, was the tongue of land falling off from the hill of the Sacsahuaman, and lying between the Huatenay and the Rodadero. Here are situated most of the remains of Inca architecture, and to this will our attention be mainly directed.

Cuzco is in latitude 13° 31' S., and longitude 72° 2' W. of

Greenwich, at an elevation of 11,380 feet above the sea. Surrounded by high and snowy mountains, it might be supposed to possess a cold not to say frigid climate; but, in fact, its temperature though cool is seldom freezing, and although in what is called the winter season—from May to November—the pastures and fields are sere, and the leaves fall from most of the trees, it is rather from drouth (for the winter is the dry season) than from frost. On the whole the climate is equable and salubrious. Wheat, barley, maize, and potatoes ripen in the valley, and the strawberry and peach are not unknown. Equalize the extremes of a Pennsylvania summer and winter, or accept the climate of the south of France, and we shall have very nearly that of Cuzco. When we add to these favorable conditions that not more than twenty miles distant are deep and hot valleys where semi-tropical fruits may be produced abundantly, we may comprehend that Cuzco was not an unfavorable site for a national capital.

From the first the seat of government and the shrine of religion, it ultimately became the centre of a polity more profound than seems to have existed among the other American nations—a polity which subordinated the military arm to the grand object of moulding the scattered tribes and petty nationalities of the Sierra into a homogeneous civil body, and of harmonizing religion so that the several blocks of the national edifice should form integral parts of a constant and durable whole.

In its very construction and the arrangement of its divisions and wards, it was made to reflect this polity. It was made a microcosm of the empire. In common with the country at large it was divided into four quarters by four roads leading to the corresponding portions of the empire, which bore the general designation of Tihuantisuya, signifying the "four quarters of the world." These roads do not run exactly in the direction of the cardinal points, as is generally affirmed, but rather intermediately; that is to say, northeast and southeast, and northwest and southwest, their direction being fixed by the conformation of the country. The division to the northwest was named Chinchasuya, and in that direction lay the second city of the empire, Quito. That to the southwest, Cuntisuya, embraced the region of the coast. That to the southeast, in the direction and including the region around Lake Titicaca, Collasuya; and that to the northeast, Antisuya.

The road running northeast and southwest bounded the great square of Cuzco on its southeast side, and divided the city in two very nearly square parts, the more elevated part in the direction of the hill and fortress of Sacsahuaman being called Hanan, or Upper Cuzco; and the lower part subsiding into the level of the valley Hurin, or Lower Cuzco. Taking the Huacapata, or central square of the old city, and which is now the Plaza Principal, as a centre, there were grouped around it, in the form of a large oval, no less than twelve subdivisions or wards. These were occupied by inhabitants from the several principal provinces of the empire, and the position of each ward was made to conform as nearly as possible to the relative position of the province of which it was the representative. The names of these wards, however, so far as they can be made out, were given entirely with reference to their actual locality, such as Cantutpata, the terrace of flowers; Pumacanchu, the place of tigers, and not with reference to their inhabitants.

Remains of the Palace of the First Inca, Cuzco

As I have said, the most important part of the sacred city was the spur of the hill of the Sacsahuaman, extending down between the rivulets Huatenay and Rodadero—a tongue of land, calculating from the terraces of the Colcompata, where the first Inca built his palace, to the confluence of the two streams, called metaphorically Pumapchupam, or the tail of the Puma, a mile in length by a quarter of a mile broad in its widest part, and comprising very nearly 130 acres. Within this area, on ground sloping to the valley in front, and to the rivulets on either hand, the royal ayllos, families or lineages, had their residences. Here were the palaces of the Incas, the buildings dedicated to instruction, the great structures in which festivals were held, the Convent of the Virgins of the Sun, and, situated far down toward the Pumapchupam, in the district called Coricanchu, or Place of Gold, the gorgeous Temple of the Sun, with its chapels sacred to the Moon, the Stars, the Thunder, and the Lightning. It was here, after the conquest, that the principal Conquistadors obtained their repartimientos of land, and on the ruins of the Inca palaces reared their own parvenu residences. Over the imposing gateways of the Inca edifices, which they preserved as entrances of their own, we still find, stuccoed in high relief, the arms of Pizarro, Almagro, Gonzalez, Quiñonez, La Vega, Valdivia, Toledo, and the other adventurers who for a while sought to emulate in pomp and display the nobles of the other, not to say higher, civilization which they had displaced. By a coincidence perhaps not wholly accidental, the Convent of Santa Catalina was established on the site, retaining in great part the very walls of the Acllahuasa or Palace of the Virgins of the Sun, and is still sacred to the vestals of another religion. The Temple of the Sun itself became the Convent of the Monks of Santo Domingo, who, in failing numbers, still prolong a sapless life among its gray and classic walls—ruin on ruin, a decadent faith expiring among the cold, dead ashes of a primitive superstition. The great Cathedral of Cuzco rises on the very spot where the eighth Inca, Viracocha, erected a building dedicated to the festivals of the people, in which a whole regiment of men could manoeuvre, and where the scant forces of Gonsalvo Pizarro found refuge in the last desperate attempt of the Peruvians to recover their lost empire and reinstate the vicegerent of the Sun. Here, according to the legend, authenticated in archaic sculpture over the doors of the Chapel of Santiago, St. James came down visibly and tangibly on his white charger, and, with lance in rest, turned the tide of battle in favor of the Spaniards, and extirpated forever the Inca power.

Inca Doorway in Cuzco.

All over this narrow tongue of land we find still the evidences of Inca greatness, as exhibited in their architecture. The streets of the new city are almost all of them defined by long reaches of walls of stones, elaborately cut, and fitting together with a precision not excelled in any of the structures of Greece or Rome, and which modern art may emulate but can not surpass. The walls of the Temple of the Sun, of the Convent of the Vestals, of the Palaces of the two Yupanquis, of Viracocha, Huayna Capac, the Inca Rocca, and portions of those of the palace attributed to the first Inca, are still preserved, and justify the most extravagant praise bestowed by old Garcilaso de la Vega and the early chroniclers on the skill of the ancient builders. But even where these walls have disappeared, and the stones which composed them have been used for other structures, we still find the ancient doorways, which the modern builders have preserved, and are thus enabled to define the outlines of the aboriginal city.

The centre of this city was the Huacapata or great public square, now covered in part, as already said, by the modern principal plaza. The ancient square, however, extended over the Huatenay, and embraced also what is now the Plaza del Cabildo, and the area covered by the block of houses between that plaza and the church and convent of La Merced. And I may here mention that both the rivulets Huatenay and Rodadero were shut in by walls of cut stone, with stairways descending, at intervals, to the water, and thus confined in narrow beds covered by bridges of a single stone, or by others composed of stones projecting from either side, and a single long stone reaching over the space between them.

Inca Bridge over the Huatenay, Cuzco

Built, as was Cuzco, on declivities more or less abrupt, the Ancient architects were obliged to resort to an elaborate system of terracing in order to obtain level areas to receive their edifices. These terraces were faced with walls, slightly inclining inward, and uniformly of the kind called "Cyclopean;" that is to say, composed of stones of irregular size and of every conceivable shape, but accurately fitted together. Where there are long lines of these walls, as for instance those supporting the terraces of the Colcampata, the monotony of the front is generally broken up by the introduction of countersunk niches, something like the blind windows, as I believe they are called, which our architects introduce to relieve the blank walls of houses. These niches are always a little narrower at the top than at the bottom, as were also nearly all the Inca doorways and windows. Inca architecture is peculiar and characteristic. Wherever it was introduced among the nations of the coast and other parts of the empire it may be at once recognized. In its massiveness, the inclination of its walls, the style of its cornices, and in some other respects, it certainly bears some resemblance to that of the ancient Egyptians; but the resemblances are not of a kind to imply necessarily either connection or intercourse between Egypt and Peru. Architectural progress must be made through the same steps and over the same road in all countries, and primitive architecture, as primitive ideas, must have a likeness.

Church and Convent of Santo Domingo, Cuzco

It is impossible within the limits of a popular article like this to give even an outline of the monuments of the old Inca metropolis, and I shall not undertake to do so; but limit myself to a brief notice of the remains of the Temple of the Sun, the principal and probably the most imposing edifice not only in Cuzco but in all Peru. The accounts of its splendor and riches left by the conquerors, and in which they have exhausted the superlatives of their grandiose language, have been so often reproduced as to be familiar to every intelligent reader.

They represent the structure as being four hundred paces in circuit; with high walls of finely cut stones, inclosing a court on which opened a number of chapels dedicated to the celestial objects of Peruvian worship, and apartments appropriated to the priests and attendants. The chronicle attributed to Sarmiento states that he never saw but two edifices in Spain comparable with it in workmanship; and Garcillaso affirms that all that was written of it by the Spaniards, and all that he could write himself, would fail to give a just idea of its greatness.

The temple proper occupied the whole of one side of the court. The principal entrance, says Garcillaso, was to the north. The cornice of the walls outside and in was of gold, or plated with gold, as were the inner walls. The roof was high and pointed, and of thatch, but the ceiling was of wood and flat. At the eastern end was a great plate of gold, representing the sun, and ranged beneath it, in royal robes and seated in golden chairs, the dessicated, some say embalmed—bodies of the Inca rulers; the body of Huayna Capac, as the greatest of the Inca line, being alone honored with a place in front of the symbol. This plate, all of one piece, spread from one wall to the other, and was the only object of worship in the building.

Surrounding the court were other separate structures dedicated respectively to the Moon, Venus, and the Pleiades, the Thunder and Lightning, and the Rainbow. There were also a large saloon for the supreme pontiff, and apartments for attendants. All these are described as having been richly decorated with gold and silver.

The existing remains confirm substantially the descriptions of the chroniclers. The site of the temple, as I have already said, is covered by the church and convent of Santo Domingo. The few ignorant but amiable friars that remain of the once rich and renowned order of Santo Domingo in Cuzco admitted me as an honorary member of their brotherhood, gave me a cell to myself, and permitted me during the week I spent with them to ransack every portion of the church, and every nook and corner of the convent, and to measure and sketch and photograph to my fill. Here a long reach of massive wall, yonder a fragment, now a corner, next a doorway, and anon a terrace — through the aid of these I was able to make up a ground-plan of the ancient edifice, substantially if not entirely accurate.

Court of the Convent of Santo Domingo, Ancient Inca Fountain

The temple proper, as described by Garcillaso, and as my own researches have proved, formed one side of a rectangular court, around which were ranged the dependent structures mentioned by him. It was not built, as has been universally alleged, so that its sides should conform to the cardinal points, but these coincided in direction with the bearings of the ancient streets, which, as I have said, were nearly at an angle of 45° with those points. Nor was its door at "one end exactly facing the east," so that the rays of the sun, when it rose, "should shine directly on its own golden image placed on the opposite wall of the temple." The entrance was on the northeast side of the building, and opened upon a square, or rather a rectangular area, called now as anciently Inti-pampa, or Field of the Sun. This is still surrounded by heavy walls of cut stones, sculptured all over with serpents in relief, on which are raised the houses of the modern inhabitants. This square was dedicated to the more solemn ceremonials of the Inca religion, and within it none dared enter except on sacred occasions, and then only with bare feet and uncovered heads.

The end of the temple next the Rio Huatenay, and that best preserved, rose above the famous Gardens of the Sun, and it is now built over by a sort of balcony, not directly connected with the modern church—a belvidere, in short. It was at this end of the temple that the great golden figure of the Sun was placed, which, falling to the lot of the Conquistador Leguizano, was gambled away before morning.

I present a view of this extremity of the ancient edifice. is circular in shape, with walls of beautifully cut and closely fitting stones, sloping gently inward. In my opinion, within this circular extremity of the temple once stood one of those stones or "columns," which, under the name of Inti-huatani, were used to designate the solstices and equinoxes, and through which the periods of planting and harvest were fixed, and the times of the great festivals determined.

The structure dedicated to the Stars was 51 feet long by 26 broad, inside the walls; and that dedicated to the Moon, and those to the Thunder, the Lightning, the Rainbow, and the Pleiades were, so far as can be made out, of about the same dimensions. The convent of the priests, or rather the apartments of the guardians of the temple, were on the right hand of the court, the observer facing northward. These apartments were 33 feet 10 inches long by 13 feet 4 inches wide, inside the walls, each entered by two doorways, and having eight niches in the wall opposite the entrances, and three at each end. The stone reservoir or fountain carved from a single blocks of which the chroniclers speak as plated over with gold, still stands in the centre of the court. It is a long octagon seven feet by four, and three feet deep. The hole in the bottom, through which the pipe entered by which it was filled, is still open; but the conduit which supplied it is destroyed. The convent, nevertheless, is still supplied by water coming through subterranean channels, the sources of which are unknown. There is some reason for believing that the Incas understood the law of fluids known as equilibrium, which the Romans did not, and carried water for supply of the temple and some of their palaces through inverted syphons, and below the bed of the Huatenay.

Remaining End Walls, Temple of the Sun, Cuzco

On the side of the Huatenay the outlook from the Temple of the Sun must have been, as it still is, very fine, bounded only by the mountains that shut in the bolson of Cuzco in that direction. On the opposite side, however, there seems to have been only a narrow street, but nine feet wide, and buildings of a comparatively rude construction. The Inti-pampa in front, entered by three streets leading between lofty walls, still high and solid, from the Huacapata

158

or Central Square, was, after all, only about 400 feet long by 100 wide, and does not realize the grandeur which the early accounts attach to it.

Side Wall of Temple of the Sun, Ancient Street, Cuzco

Some of the chronicles speak of the temple as being surrounded by a high wall; whereas nothing is more certain than that the exterior walls were simply those of the edifice itself. They tell us also that the terraces which formed the garden of the temple were covered with golden clods, and supported an infinite variety of trees and vegetables imitated in gold and silver, with figures of men, animals, birds, reptiles, and insects, all in the same precious metals. That the inner walls of the temple were covered with these metals, and that the inner and outer cornice, a yard broad, as Garcillaso says, were of gold, is not incredible; but that the gardens of the temple, extending over an area 600 feet long by nearly 300 broad, were thus covered with gold and silver exceeds belief. Not that the ancient smiths did not sometimes imitate natural objects with considerable skill, for of this we have abundant evidence, but because the Incas seem to have been a race of remarkably good sense, and eminently practical and utilitarian in their notions and practices —too much so, I am induced to believe, to have gold worked up in imitation of firewood, and piled away in the temple!

There exists in Cuzco, in some of the private museums, portions of the golden plates with which the walls of the Temple of the Sun were covered. There is hardly a doubt of their authenticity. They are simple sheets of pure gold, beaten exceedingly thin, not thicker than fine note-paper.

A conspicuous object from every part of Cuzco is the steep, overhanging hill of the Sacsahuaman, rising to the height of 760 feet to the north of the city, and on which the Incas raised that gigantic, Cyclopean fortress denominated by the conquerors the ninth great wonder of the world. I shall have occasion to describe this fortress in another place; but at present refer to it only to say that well up on its Jidda or slope, just at the point where it becomes so steep as almost to render ascent impossible, are a series of elaborate terraces, supported by Cyclopean wall, ornamented with niches, and called the Colcompata, or Terrace of the Granaries. It was here, it is said, that, the first Inca, Manco Capac, the founder of Cuzco, built his palace, some fragments of which still remain—a doorway, a window, and a short section of wall, with some portions of foundations, but not enough to enable us to make out a complete plan of the structure. There were fountains here, and the site, now occupied in part by the church and plaza of San Cristobal, not only dominated the whole city but the entire valley of Cuzco. The terraces were filled in with richest soil, still celebrated for its fertility, and altogether it was and yet is almost regal in its position. The Incas were the heads of a great nation, dependent on agriculture. To evince their respect for the art lying at the foundation of their state, to elevate and dignify labor, they were wont to initiate here with their own hands the seasons of planting and of harvest. With pomp and ceremony, when the season of sowing came around, and the appropriate festivals had been celebrated, the Inca himself went to the terraces of the Colcompata, and with a golden adze, commenced to break up the soil. And when the crops of maize and quinua had ripened, he again went to the Colcompata and plucked the first ears of the harvest. The crops gathered here, under the direct cultivation of the Son of the Sun, were regarded as sacred, and, like the seeds from the holy Island of Titicaca, were distributed to be sown in the lands, dedicated to the Sun throughout the Empire. Thus carefully were the people taught that the beneficence of their deity was perpetuated through his children, and thus were they led to look up to him, through the Incas, as the impersonations of his goodness and mercy, as well as of his power.

View of the Hill of the Sacsahuaman from The Plaza Del Cabildo, Cuzco

I can not dismiss ancient Cuzco without a few words regarding its pristine state and importance, as inferable from its monuments. All students of American early history and archeology are well aware that the Spaniards never erred in underrating their enemies in story, whatever they may have done in fact. Neither Cortéz, nor Alvarado, nor Pizarro, ever encountered inferior numbers in their wars. The hosts that confronted the Union armies at Bull Run and some other places, and that led President Lincoln to affirm, as the result, of the best information he could get from his generals, that the Southern army was made of "nigh on two million of men," were insignificant, numerically, as compared with those that the conquistadors tell us they encountered. We know that Leonidas fought in the shadow of the hurtling arrows of the Persians; but the legions of Xerxes were small and few as compared with those that the Spaniards had to meet in America—that is to say, if we take their relations literally. The cities they conquered were always grand and populous, and the state of their princes dazzling, even to men who had seen the Alhambra and knew from historic poetry the glories of the Moors. In many, perhaps in most, respects—it may be in all—Cuzco was the most impressive city they had found in all the Americas. That it had barbaric wealth of gold and silver, and stately structures, we can well believe; for this is confirmed by concurrent evidence and existing remains. But that it ever contained much more than its existing population appears to me improbable. The story that it held 200,000 inhabitants, and that as many more lived in its suburbs, is simply incredible. The houses of the common people of the Sierra, and in the region around Cuzco, were not built, as are those of Central America and Mexico, of canes and other materials that might disappear in a single season, but of stone or adobes, that could not fail to leave some enduring traces. Such traces do not exist around Cuzco; and however great may have been the concurrence there on important occasions, when the people gathered from the valleys of Yucay and Paucurtambo, from the bolsons of Andahuaylillas and Xaxiguana, the puns of Chinchero and Chita, and from all the quarters of a mighty empire, yet it does not seem probable that the city ever possessed a permanent population of more than 50,000, while another equal number were dispersed through its valley.

The department of Cuzco is now the most populous of Peru, its inhabitants numbering upward of 300,000. These exhaust very nearly all its resources; and even if we concede that the economies of agriculture are less now than in ancient times, we must remember that the horse, the ox, the sheep, the goat, the pig, a number of vegetables, wheat and barley, have all been introduced since the conquest, and have contributed their aid to the support of population.

I can not agree with those writers who speak of the aspect of ancient Cuzco as bright and shining, and gay with many tints. Its most imposing edifices were, as we have seen, built of trachyte of sombre color. These clearly were neither stuccoed nor painted. The residences of the people, built of rough stones laid in clay, were probably stuccoed and painted yellow and red, and may have given some appearance of lightness to the city. The domes and towers of which we sometimes read probably never existed; those architectural terms being oftenest used in loose descriptions, framed on Oriental models, and intended to be impressive rather than accurate. Nor was the city laid out with perfect regularity, the streets crossing each other at right angles. Nor were the banks of the Huatenay faced with stones for a distance of twenty leagues, but simply for the distance it flowed through the city.

Religious Procession and Church of La Merced, Cuzco

Modern Cuzco extends very compactly over the entire space between the Huatenay and Almodena, and even past the latter stream, forming the barrio of Belen. Although considerably reduced in population since the Independence, it still numbers not far from 40,000 inhabitants, and, as the capital of the Department of the same name, is, necessarily, a place of some importance—the seat of a Bishopric and a University, a Prefecture and a garrison. It is very well built, the edifices being mainly those raised by the conquerors themselves in the height of their wealth and activity, when they had mitas and repartimientos, before the treasures collected through five centuries had been scattered, and while they had a large, industrious, and skillful population under their absolute control. In style eminently Moorish, the houses are built around courts, with open corridors, supported by delicate columns, into which open the apartments of every story. Jalousies project from the fronts, and the whole aspect of the place is that of Granada in Spain. The lower or ground floor of the best buildings, facing on the principal streets, are cut up in small, dark rooms, without windows, which are the shops, smitheries, picanterias, etc., of the town. The churches and convents are numerous and extensive. Of the former there are thirty, and of the latter eleven, five of which have been suppressed. They are all remarkably well built. The Cathedral, fronting on the principal square, is a large, massive, and rather heavy structure; but the Church of the Jesuits, fronting on the same square, is a marvel of architectural beauty — a little too florid, perhaps, but with the finest façade of any church I have seen in America. The tower of the Church of La Merced is admirable in proportion and taste, and the courts of the convent of the same name are surrounded by colonnades of white stone, elaborately carved, and which in grace and harmony may challenge comparison with the finest of Italy. Within this church lie the remains of Juan and Gonsalvo Pizarro and Almagro. Both churches and convents are crowded with pictures, some of merit and historical value. Of the latter there is a series in the little church of Santa Ana, contemporaneous with the conquest. They illustrate the procession of Corpus Christi, in which the Incarial family, in regal native costume, take part. Among them is Paullu, younger son of the great Huayna Capac, and numerous ñustas or princesses, the daughters and nieces of the same monarch. As illustrating the costumes and customs of the period these paintings have singular interest, and deserve to be faithfully copied.

For many years after the conquest, and long after Lima was founded, Cuzco continued to be the chief city of Peru, the seat of its wealth and learning, and the residence of its most noble families. But as the roads of the Incas fell into decay, the difficulties of reaching it, always great, were augmented, and the Viceregal Court established in Lima, more corrupt and luxurious than any in America, gradually drew away its more enterprising and ambitious inhabitants. Infinitely less is known of Cuzco in Lima, today, than of Berlin; not one person in the capital has visited it, while a hundred have visited Paris; and the journey from Lima to New York may be made in less time, at a fourth of the cost, and a thousandth part of the trouble and fatigue, than it can be made from the same point to the proud but isolated city of the Sierra. I know of but two American travelers besides myself who have visited it, Mr. S. G. Arnold, of Rhode Island, and Lieutenant Gibbon, of the United States Navy—the latter, only, publishing any account of his visit. I have only to add that seven-eighths of the population of Cuzco are pure Indians, and that a knowledge of Quichua is almost absolutely necessary for open intercourse with the mass of its inhabitants.

The Fourth of July in Peru occurs on the 28th, that being the anniversary of Peruvian Independence, and it came around on the second day after our arrival in Cuzco. It was ushered in by the same sulphurous detonations that we are accustomed to at home on similar occasions, and there was a review of the garrison and the volunteer militia, a concurrence of the notables of the city at the Cathedral, with a discourse from one of the canonigos, in which he reflected on the government, and was arrested for his pains in the evening. The students in the University, patriotic as students always are, were the most active participants in the festivities of the day—all dressed in black tail-coats, with funny cocked hats, like the dives of St. Cyr in Paris. They constituted the leading feature in the procession in the afternoon, dragging with them through the streets a radiant Goddess of Freedom, in the shape of a huge doll with flaxen ringlets and a liberty cap, glittering with tinsel, and mounted on two wheels borrowed for the occasion from the only piece of artillery which a prudent government intrusts to the rather turbulent citizens of Cuzco. The Indians looked on with an indifferent air, as a matter that little concerned them, and only drank a little more chicha than usual. The great excitement of the day was the explosion of a keg of gunpowder in the cuartel or barracks, which are the sequestered cloisters of the Jesuits, where a squad of soldiers were compounding fireworks for the evening, resulting in killing four or five, and mangling or horribly burning twenty or thirty more—a practical commentary on the general impolicy of men smoking cigars in a powder magazine. In the centre of the great plaza was raised a symbolical monument, a sort of Temple of Liberty, made of canvas, stretched on frames, in which were portraits of the Benemeritos of Freedom in all parts of the world—Lincoln and Garibaldi side by side.

The students were not satisfied with the performances of the day, but insisted on prolonging them by a procession by moonlight, in which it was proposed I should carry the Peruvian flag, supported on each side by that of the United States. My Puno experiences were too recent to make me ambitious of the distinction; but the students invaded the courtyard of the commandante's house in a body, dragging the Goddess with them, and refused to credit my assurances of indisposition and Col. Vargas's more truthful asseveration that we were tired out and wanted rest. Finally a compromise was effected, and I consented to be standard-bearer, but only through the plaza and as far as the Alameda. The announcement was received with tumultuous vivas for the United States, which a single indiscreet individual sought to oppose with some allusion to Mr. Webster's *faux pas* in the Lobos Islands business. This resulted in the dissentient getting so savagely handled that he was obliged to keep his bed for many weeks after.

The white and foreign population of Cuzco is small, made up chiefly of government officials, a few wealthy haciendados, who live a great part of the time on their estates, and a dozen small comerciantes, who would be called shop-keepers in any other country. Collectively these are so few as hardly to be appreciable in the streets, and the aspect of the place is therefore that of a thoroughly Indian town. There is hardly anything that can be called society, although the better class is hospitable and unaffected, and much more frank and easy in manner than the corresponding class in the towns of the coast, where native manners have been sacrificed in a vain attempt to imitate "foreign airs and graces."

Some of the old families live in considerable style, and their houses are fitted with real elegance. A few of them retain apartments with heavy damask and embroidered hangings, and the rich and massive furniture and carvings of two hundred years ago, when the nobility and wealth of Peru was concentrated in Cuzco. Others are furnished in modern, thoroughly French style, with great mirrors, inlaid wardrobes, and grand pianos, that have been brought up, with infinite labor and at almost fabulous cost, on men's shoulders, from the coast.

I may refer particularly to the residence of a lady who lives on the Plaza of San Francisco, whose attention to strangers is proverbial, and who has established an honorable public reputation as the collector of the finest and most valuable collection of antiquities in Peru, the Señora Zentino. This house would be called a palace even in Venice, if not in architecture, certainly in extent. In the spaciousness of its apartments, and their rich and varied contents and decorations, it would creditably compare with some of the finest on the Grand Canal. An adequate description of the museum would occupy a volume, and I content myself with engravings of some pieces of pottery selected from many hundreds, illustrating the skill of the ancients in the plastic arts, and their appreciation of humor.

In some respects the most important relic in Senora Zentino's collection is the frontal bone of a skull, from the Inca cemetery in the valley of Yucay, which exhibits a clear case of trepanning before death. The Senora was kind enough to intrust it to me for investigation, and it has been submitted to the criticism of the best surgeons of the United States and Europe, and regarded by all as the most remarkable evidence of a knowledge of surgery among the aborigines yet discovered on this continent; for trepanning is one of the most difficult of surgical processes. The cutting through the bone was not performed with a saw, but evidently with a burin or tool like that used by engravers on wood and metal. The opening is 58 hundredths of an inch wide and 70 hundredths long.

The absence of sculptures in Peru, except of small articles in stone, is conspicuous, and quite in contrast with what we find in Central America and Mexico. Except figures of serpents in relief on walls and lintels, and a single group of tigers over the doors of a house in the Calle de Santa Ana, there are no sculptures to be seen in Cuzco. There are some figures resembling griffins, etc., in the court of a house in the Calle del Triunfo, and a so-called siren built in the terrace wall of the Colcompata; but I regard them as modern. In the collection of the Señora Zentino, however, are two stone figures, rudely resembling tigers, which, it is said, were taken from the Gardens of the Sun, where they stood one on each side the stairway that led from up the terraces. The bases are cut in such a way as to favor the hypothesis that they were built in some sort of wall, perhaps in the coping. Each is two feet high.

Ancient Stone Sculpure, Cuzco

Among the notable objects of interest in Cuzco is the Alameda, to the south of the town, on the banks of the Huatenay, and opposite the ancient Gardens of the Sun. This is a long and rather narrow area, planted with willows and alder-trees, laid out with some taste, and having a kind of Grecian temple and a colonnade at its further extremity. But nobody walks there, and it is grown up with cactuses and weeds, over which the wash-women from the neighboring stream spread their clothes to dry. Public spirit in Peru is spasmodic, and all works of embellishment excite only a momentary interest, and then succumb under the general apathy of the people. The sentiment of affection does something to keep the various panteones or cemeteries in decent condition, and that of Cuzco is tasteful and well ordered. But it strikes the visitor as strange that, with such a vast expanse of earth open to receive and protect forever the remains of the dead, they should be thrust for only a year or two in ovens in the walls, and then dragged out and burned or buried in a corner.

My first visit to the Panteon of Cuzco was early in the morning, and as I approached the barrio of Belen, outside the city, in which it stands, I observed a funeral procession in the street before me, preceded by some men carrying candles, a man playing a violin, and another a clarionet. As they passed the various squalid houses in that quarter the women rushed out with disheveled hair, and, huddling behind the bier, commenced the loudest and most extravagant wailings of which the human organs are capable. I was astonished at such violence of grief, and wondered who had died that had so deep a hold on the popular sympathies. I overtook the procession, or rather huddle, at the bridge of the Almodena, where suddenly the lamentations ceased, and the inconsolables clustered eagerly around a man, who, standing on a block of stone, distributed cuartillos (three-cent pieces) to them from his hat, whereupon, chatting and laughing, the afflicted creatures turned back to await another funeral. For a medio each these professional weepers of the Calle del Hospital will accompany the corpse to the gate of the cemetery, break their very hearts with grief, and dissolve themselves in tears.

Terra Cottas Cuzco

The Panteon is shut in by high white walls, and entered beneath a lofty stone gateway, with trellised iron doors, over which is a deep niche, wherein stands a veritable skeleton, supported by an iron rod, wearing a gilt crown on its bony head, and holding in its fleshless hands two banners of sheet metal, one of which bears the inscription:

YO SOY PABLO BILIACA,

"I am Paul Biliaca;" and the other,

MEMENTO MORI.

Pablo Biliaca was a mason, and had been killed by a fall while repairing the front of the Cathedral.

The recreations of Cuzco are religious processions and cockfighting; the former "coming off" almost daily, and so frequently that I early ceased to inquire about them. The latter occur only on Sundays. The cancha or cockpit is in the court of the old suppressed beatario of San Andres, and consists of a raised ring of mud two feet high and as many thick, surrounded by other rings of graduated height, as seats for the spectators. Around the court are tiers of coops for the cocks, some of which were piled full of skulls and bones of the devout beatas, who had died here and been buried in the court, the earth of which, including their own dust, had been dug up to form the wells of the cancha. The fights were well attended by the clergy, the judiciary, and the military. I had the good fortune to win an onza from the judge of the Supreme Court, who challenged me to bet on the viscacha, an imported cock, with a single spur, which had already won two battles. My servant Ignacio had discovered "a bird" of excellent points in Cache, and had brought him thence wrapped up in his poncho, with a view of matching him in Cuzco. For two weeks he had shared Ignacio's apartment and absorbed most of his care, besides vexing us with his incessant crowing, so that I insisted he should fight soon, be sent away, or decapitated. Ignacio determined on the first alternative, begged a month's pay in advance, matched him for four ounces, won, then sold him for another ounce, got drunk, gambled away every cuartillo, absented himself for three days, and then came home with a swollen eye and "very bad in his head."

The dog-laws are strict and severely enforced in Cuzco, which would be overrun with mangy curs if they were not rigorously slain. The day of slaughter is Thursday of each week, when decent dogs are confined by their owners in case they do not find out, as many of them do, that the day is a black one for dogs, and stay at home of their own accord. Our host had a fine Newfoundland who understood the danger and the day, and from his safe position on the balcony, would abuse and malign the dog-killers on their appearance with all the vigor of which the canine language is capable. Woe to any one of them who undertook to enter the court of his castle on that day or any other.

Dog Killing in front of Convent of Santa Ana, Cuzco

The process of slaughter that is practiced is novel. Two Indians, each holding an end of a rope, station themselves at the mouth of a street, while two others, armed with clubs, start from its other extremity, and drive all the vagrant dogs before them. As these attempt to pass over the rope which lies harmlessly enough on the ground, it is suddenly and dextrously straightened out and the dog thrown high in the air. He is generally stunned or disabled by his fall, and dispatched by the club-bearers. I am sorry to say that even then he does not always cease to be a nuisance, as he is too often thrown into the bed of the Huatenay, which is the receptacle of all kinds of filth and rubbish, and there left to poison the air in his decay.

Of the filth of Cuzco every visitor must have sickening

recollections. It offends the eye as well as the nose, and reeks every where. The azequias in the centre of the streets are scantily supplied with water during the dry season; and as they receive all the slops and wash of the houses, they are often fetid, and all the more so as that tropical scavenger, the ordinary buzzard, never ventures into this lofty region. Probably the world has no more extraordinary spectacle than is afforded on the banks of these azequias in the early morning —certainly none more startling to the eyes of the stranger accustomed to the decencies of life.

We passed some months in Cuzco, making it the centre of our explorations in every direction around. Upward of a week was spent in effecting a careful survey of the great fortress of the Sacsahuaman, and three weeks more were occupied in the beautiful semi-tropical Valley of Yucay, where the Incas had their country seat, and in examining the ancient fortresses of Ollantaytambo and Pisac, the bulwarks of the Inca Empire on the side of the Amazon.

FORTRESSES AND GARDENS.

View in the Plaza Del Cabildo, Cuzco, Peru

THE capital of the Inca empire was not defended by walls such as protected some of the ancient Inca cities. Its valley, surrounded by high mountains, was, in itself, naturally almost impregnable, and the approaches to it were covered by fortifications. But the city, nevertheless, had its citadel or fortress, dominating it as the Acropolis did Athens, Ehrenbreitstein the villages at its foot, the Castle, Edinburgh, and "the Rock," Gibraltar. It was built upon the bold headland projecting into the valley of Cuzco between the rivulets Huatenay and Rodadero, looking from below like a high abrupt hill, but being really only the spur of a shelf or plateau, somewhat irregular in surface, which in turn is commanded by higher hills, or apparent hills or mountains, themselves the escarpments of remoter natural terraces or puna lands. This headland is called los Altos del Sacsahuaman, the latter being a compound word signifying, "Fill thee, falcon!" or, "Gorge thyself, hawk!"

173

Thus metaphorically did the Incas glorify the strength of their fortress. "Dash thyself against its rocky and impregnable sides, if thou wilt; the hawks will gather up thy fragments!" Vainglorious and proud were those ancients, as the nations who today call their war vessels the Invincible, the Devastation, and the Scourge.

On the side of the city the eminence of the Sacsahuaman presents a steep front, difficult and almost impossible of ascent. Up this front, and from the terraces of the Colcompata, led anciently as now a zig-zag road, ascending in places by stone steps to a series of terraces on the most projecting and commanding portion of the headland. On the uppermost of these, most conspicuous of all objects around Cuzco, on the site of an ancient building of which only a part of the foundations remains, stand three crosses: the Calvario of the city. These crosses are 764 feet above the level of the Huacapata, or modern plaza.

The usual ascent to the Sacsahuaman, and which is practicable by horses, is through the gorge or ravine of the Rodadero, to the right of the eminence, where a road is partly cut out of the hill and partly built up against it—a cliff on one side and a precipice on the other. At the bottom of the ravine the little Rodadero chafes and murmurs, here leaping, a miniature cataract, from one shelf to another; and next gathering in dark, shaded, bubble-covered pools, as if recovering courage for another plunge. In ascending the Sacsahuaman we will start from the foot of the street of el Triunfo, where it rests on the rivulet Rodadero, or Tullamayo, and then turn to the left. Leaving the Cyclopean terrace of the Inca Roca behind us, we pass in front of the Yachahuasi, or schools erected by that patron of learning. It seems to have been a vast building, or series of buildings, several hundred feet in length, with walls of relatively small but perfectly fitting stones, which enter largely into the modern structures. After passing a few blocks we come to the gorge of the Rodadero, where it is traversed by a modern aqueduct built on arches, between an abutment of rock on one side and of ancient Inca work on the other—a picturesque and pleasing object. A short, sharp scramble and we reach one of the lower terraces of the Colcompata, and the road proper to the Sacsahuaman. We pass in succession the upper and lower falls of the Rodadero, which mingle the tinkle and murmur of their waters with those of the azequias that flow in invisible channels above our heads. We will require to stop frequently in open spaces, left for the purpose, either to recover breath or permit our animals to do so, as well as to allow the troops of llamas, led by their silent owners down the rugged pathway, to pass us.

Aqueduct Over the Tullamay or Rodardero

At one point we discover what appears to be a well, or square shaft, walled in with cut stones, fourteen feet deep. The wall on the inner aide, or that lying next the slope, is also sloping, as if to facilitate the passage of water. The bottom of the shaft is filled with rubbish, and without excavation it is impossible to say whither it leads. It is probably part of one of the subterranean aqueducts through which the Incas conducted water into their capital from distant, and often unknown sources.

As we ascend, we observe, high up above us on our left, long lines of walls, which are the faces of the eastern terraces of the Fortress. These become heavier as we advance until, when we finally reach the level of the plateau, up the rugged front of which we have been struggling, they cease to be simply retaining-walls, and rise in massive, independent walls composed of great blocks of limestone. A gateway, flanked by heavy stones, opens on our left, and we stop while a drove of llamas defile through it. Stone steps formerly existed by which to ascend to the higher grounds within, but they have been broken away, although their traces remain. It was in attempting to force this gateway, in the last desperate encounter between the Spaniards and the Incas, that Juan Pizarro, the brother of the conqueror, was killed.

Upper Fall of the Rodadero

Passing through this gateway—the ancient Tiupuncu, or "Gate of Sand"—and through the main outer walls of the Fortress, we find ourselves in a little open plain or pampa. On our right we notice a considerable eminence of rock of singular aspect, called el Rodadero, and on the other hand we have our first view of the great

Cyclopean walls of the Fortress of the Sacsahuaman—the most massive among monuments of similar character, either in the Old or New Worlds.

Before attempting to describe this vast structure I should explain that the mass of the headland on which the Fortress stands is a metamorphic rock, disintegrating, hard in parts and soft in others, thrust up by igneous action from below, and bearing on its surface huge fragments of limestone from adjacent cliffs of that material—a tumultuous piece of natural workmanship which it would require an accomplished geologist to classify and explain. This headland is highest where it overlooks the city, and behind it is the area or pampa to which I have alluded, perhaps a hundred feet lower than its loftiest point—an area unquestionably much leveled by art, and now smooth as a prairie. Beyond this, and about three hundred feet distant, is the swell of amphibolic rock called the Rodadero, to which I have also alluded, and of which I shall have occasion to speak further on.

But before going on let us see what the chroniclers have to say concerning the work within which we are now standing. It elicited from them an admiration scarcely less extravagant than was bestowed on the Temple of the Sun: "This was the greatest and most superb of the edifices," says Garcillaso de la Vega, "that the Incas raised to demonstrate their majesty and power. Its greatness is incredible to those who have not seen it; and those who have seen it and studied it with attention, will be led not alone to imagine but to believe that it was reared by enchantment, by demons and not by men, because of the number and size of the stones placed in the three walls, which are rather cliffs than walls, and which it is impossible to believe were cut out of quarries, since the Indians had neither iron nor steel wherewith to extract or shape them. And how they were brought together is a thing equally wonderful, since the Indians had neither carts nor oxen nor ropes wherewith to drag them by main force. Nor were there level roads over which to transport them, but, on the contrary, steep mountains and abrupt declivities, to be overcome by the simple force of men. Many of the stones were brought," continues the chronicler, "from ten to fifteen leagues, and especially the stone, or rather the rock, called Saycusca, or the Tired

Stone, because it never reached the structure, and which it is known was brought a distance of fifteen leagues, from beyond the river of Yucay, which is little less in size than the Guadalquivir at Cordova. The stones obtained nearest were from Muyna, five leagues from Cuzco. It passes the power of imagination to conceive how so many and so great stones could be so accurately fitted together as scarcely to admit the insertion of the point of a knife between them. Many are indeed so well fitted that the joint can hardly be discovered. And all this is the more wonderful as they had no squares or levels to place on the stones and ascertain if they would fit together. How often must they have taken up and put down the stones to ascertain if the joints were perfect? Nor did they have cranes, nor pulleys, nor other machinery whatever. But what is most marvelous of the edifice is the incredible size of the stones, and the astonishing labor of bringing them together and placing them."

Lower Fall of The Rodadero

Here Garcillaso proceeds to quote Acosta, "because he had not received such clear and exact measurements of the stones of the Fortress of Cuzco as he had asked for." Acosta says that he measured stones in Tiahuanaco "thirty feet long, eighteen broad, and six thick;" but that in the Fortress of Cuzco are others much larger, "and much to be admired, because, although irregular in size and shape, they were nevertheless perfectly joined, each stone fitting into the other as if made for the place."

The outline of the eminence of the Sacsahuaman, on the side toward the rocks of the Rodadero, is rather concave than otherwise, and it is along this face that the heaviest works of the Fortress were built. They remain substantially perfect, and will remain so—unless disturbed by a violence which is not to be anticipated, and of which the present inhabitants of Cuzco hardly seem capable—as long as the Pyramids shall last, or Stonehenge and the Colosseum shall endure, for it is only with these works that the Fortress of the Sacsahuaman can be properly compared.

Part of Inca Aqueduct

The defenses consist, on this side, of three lines of massive walls, each supporting a terrace and parapet. The walls are nearly parallel, and have approximately accurate entering and reentering angles for their total existing length of 1800 feet. The first or outer wall has an average present height of 27 feet; the second wall is 35 feet within it, and is 18 feet high; the third is 18 feet within the second, and is, in its highest part, 14 feet in elevation. The total elevation of the works is therefore 59 feet.

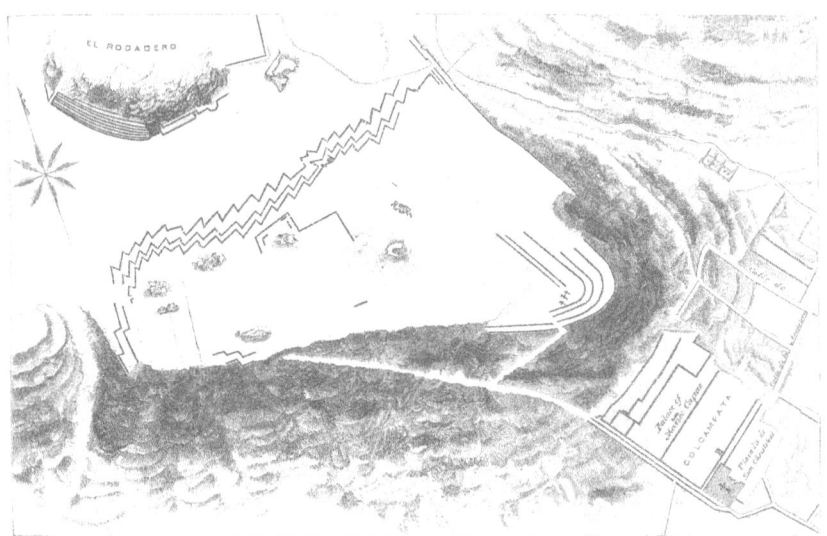

Plan of the Inca Fortress of the Sacsahuaman, Dominating the City of Cuzco.

I am now speaking strictly of the walls on the northern front of the Fortress. Long lines of wall extend along the heights dominating the gorge of the rivulet Rodadero; and there are sections of walls, besides those of the terraces of the Calvario, on the brow of the hill on the side of the city. As these were constructed of regularly squared stones, they have been almost wholly destroyed, the stones having been rolled down the eminence to enter into the walls of the numerous churches and convents of the modern town.

The remarkable feature of the walls of the Fortress, on its only assailable side, is the conformation with modern defensive structures in the employment of salients, so that the entire face of the walls could be covered by a parallel fire from the weapons of the defenders. This feature is not the result in any degree of the conformation of the ground, but of a clearly settled plan. The stones composing the walls are massive blocks of blue limestone, irregular in size and shape, and the work is altogether without doubt the grandest specimen of the style called "Cyclopean" extant in America. The outer wall, as I have said, is heaviest.

Each salient terminates in an immense block of stone, sometimes as high as the level of the terrace which it supports, but generally sustaining one or more great stones only less in size than itself. One of these stones is 27 feet high, 14 broad, and 12 in thickness. Stones of 15 feet length, 12 in width, and 10 in thickness, are common in the outer walls. They are all slightly beveled on the face, and near the joints chamfered down sharply to the contiguous faces. The joints—what with the lapse of time, and under the effects of violence, earthquakes, and the weather—are not now, if they ever were, as perfect as represented by the chroniclers. They are, nevertheless, wonderfully close, and cut with a precision rarely seen in modern fortifications. The inner walls are composed of smaller and more regular stones, and are less impressive.

Each wall supports a terrace or platform, filled in, as we discovered in the excavations made by treasure seekers, with large, rough stones and the chippings of those composing the walls. The Summit of each wall rose originally from six to eight feet above the level of the terrace, forming a parapet with an interior bench or step whereon the defenders might mount to discharge their missiles against assailants. To prevent accumulations of water behind the walls, the builders cut small drains or conduits through the stones at every second angle near the base of the structure—a common feature in all their terrace and retaining walls. The inner or re-entering angles were not wholly formed by the junction or placing together of blocks of stone. Here, too, the device common, in many of their more regular structures was adopted, of chiseling the angle in the stone, so that one end of the block should enter on the face of the next salient, thus "binding" the corner.

It is impossible to conceive the variety of shapes of the stones, especially of those of the outer wall, which, as Garcillaso says, "is composed of rocks rather than of stones." In some cases two immense stones, from fourteen to fifteen feet high, and ten to twelve broad, will be found placed only a foot and a half or two feet apart, with a thin slab of corresponding height cut to fit accurately between them. In other cases the upper part of a stone will be concave, and the lower a sharp angle, but each surface matching that which it adjoins.

The extremities of the heavy walls under notice have been much destroyed; but there is evidence that there were entrances or passages at each end, as well as three gateways in the main front. The chroniclers speak only of three, called respectively Tiupuncu, "the Sand Gate;" Acahuana-puncu, "the Gate of Acahuana," who was one of the engineers employed in the construction of the work, and the third Viracocha-puncu, "the Gate of Viracocha." The main entrance was rather to the left of the centre of the line of walls, where one salient was omitted, so as to leave a rectangular space, sixty-three feet long by twenty-five I broad. In the centre of the left-hand end of this space, between two blocks of stone, the outer one forming the angle being fifteen feet long, nine feet thick, and twelve high, was left an opening four feet wide. Steps led through this opening to the level of the inner terrace, the passage being lined with heavy stones. The chroniclers affirm that these openings, in times of danger, were closed by great blocks of stone, which are yet to be found near some of them, and for the reception of which we notice one step omitted on the inner side of the wall.

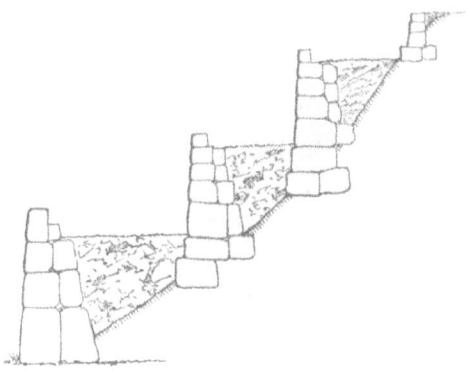

Section of the Walls of the Fortress

The entrance through the second wall at this point is more intricate, and opens against a transverse wall, where the steps turn at right angles, and thus reach the second terrace. The third wall has two entrances, one plain, like that through the first, and the second corresponding with that through the intermediate wall. The lesser entrances to the right and left of the principal ones just described, are simple openings, occurring not opposite each other, but in the alternating salients.

The easternmost gateway of all, through the parallel walls running at right angles to the general line of fortifications, is very nearly perfect, and shows the stairway very clearly. It has ten steps, each ten inches high and twelve inches broad.

The ground within the walls rises to a further elevation of about sixty feet, and is rocky. Several masses of metamorphic rock and limestone project above the soil or are scattered over it. In one of these a cavern forty feet deep has been excavated, and others are cut into steps and seats. Here are fragments of the foundations of considerable structures, of regularly cut stones, but of which the plans can not now be made out. These are probably the remnants of what the chroniclers describe as three small fortresses, or citadels, within the greater work. Two of these are said to have been square and one round. The latter was the largest and in the centre, and was called Muyuc-Marca, or "Round Building," and was designed to receive the Inca and his family in case of danger, together with the wealth of his palaces and the treasures of the Sun. It is said to have been rich in decoration, and lined with gold and silver. This is also said to have communicated by subterranean passages with the two square towers, destined for the reception of the garrison of the fortress, and with the royal palaces and the Temple of the Sun. I can credit the former part of the statement, for there are remains of such passages, but that any of these descended, as they must have done, almost vertically for 764 feet, and then horizontally into the city, is a presumption altogether improbable.

Prescott has, given the name of "The Fortress" to the three towers or citadels, and mistakes in supposing that there were but two lines of walls protecting approach to them from the side opposite the city. This is the more surprising, as Garcillaso, and others distinctly state that there were three walls, and that these constituted "The Fortress," which they regarded as the eighth wonder of the world.

As I have said, it was in a desperate attempt to recover this Fortress from the revolted Indians, that Juan Pizarro was mortally wounded, and it was from the battlements of the Muyuc-Marca that the Inca commander hurled himself to the ground when the issue of battle was decided against him. His was the last blow struck in behalf of the Inca power

Part of the Fortress of the Sacsahuaman, From "The Seat of the Inca"

The stones composing the Fortress of the Sacsahuaman are limestone, and masses of the same still lie within the walls of the Fortress, and are scattered over the plateau behind it. That some of these in the wall were taken from their natural positions near the place where they now stand is most probable; but that others were brought from the limestone cliffs that edge the plateau, three-fourths of a mile to a mile distant is certain. Two distinct, well-graded roads still remain leading to these ledges, where the evidences of quarrying are as clear as they are at Quincy, in Massachusetts. The rock is the cliff limestone, evidently considerably changed and fissured by igneous action, splitting off in great, irregular blocks, in turn much seamed and furrowed by the elements. The earth and debris were excavated away beneath these, and when they fell by their own gravity they were partly hewn on the spot, dragged to the Fortress, and there fitted. Blocks half-hewn still lie in the quarries, and some in nearly perfect condition by the side of the roads to which I have referred. How they were thus dragged we can only infer from the undoubted fact that the Incas had no draft animals. They must, therefore, have been moved by combined human force on rollers of wood or stone, and forced up inclined planes to the positions they were to occupy.. If the force of a thousand men was insufficient to move them, it was quite within the power of the Incas to bring ten times that number to the task. The Incas had both ropes and cables, and I have seen nothing in the size of the stones here or elsewhere not amenable to the power of numbers. It is not to be supposed for an instant that limestone masses should be brought from beyond the Yucay, fifteen leagues distant, when precisely the same stone was to be had near at hand in inexhaustible quantities.

Salient Angle of Fortress

The great Piedra Cansada, "Tired Stone," or Sayacusca, of which Garcillaso and others speak as having occupied 20,000 men in moving it, and which; rolling over, killed 300 workmen, is an enormous mass of a thousand tons or more, and certainly was never moved ever so slightly by human power. Its top, like the tops of hundreds of other rocks on the plateau of the Rodadero, is cut into what appear to be seats and reservoirs of every shape; its sides are cut in niches and stairways—the whole a maze of incomprehensible sculpture and of apparently idle although elaborate workmanship. The largest stone in the Fortress has a computed weight of 361 tons.

View of Cuzco and the Nevada of Asungato From The Brow of Sacsahuaman.

Three hundred feet in front of the Fortress is a dome-shaped mass of trachytic rock called el Rodadero, which, on the side toward the Fortress, was faced up in terraces with large and beautifully cut stones, which have been removed and tiled down into the city. This rock is also called la Piedra Lisa, inasmuch as its convex surface is grooved, as if the rock had been squeezed up in a plastic state between irregular and unyielding walls, and then hardened into shape with a smooth and glassy surface. A mass of dough forced up under the outspread hands would give something of the same appearance in miniature. It is said that the Inca youth amused themselves in coursing through these polished grooves on festival days—a custom which the youth of Cuzco have not allowed to fall into disuse. And here I may allude to a very comical mistake into which Rivero and Von Tschudi, together with their translators, have fallen regarding this rock. Misled by the designation "Rodadero" they have described this eminence, which is more than half a mile in circumference and at least eighty feet high, as follows: "A short distance from the Fortress is a large piece of amphibolic rock, known by the name of the Smooth Rolling Stone, which served, and still serves, for diversion to the inhabitants, by rolling like a garden roller, having a sort of hollow formed in the middle through friction!"

On the very summit of the rock of the Rodadero there are a series of broad seats, rising one above the other in front and laterally, like a stairway, cut with unsurpassable precision in the hard rock. This is called "The Seat of the Inca," and tradition relates that it was here the Incas came at intervals, through three reigns, to watch the progress of constructing the Fortress. There are other smaller seats lower down, which, the same authority relates, were occupied by the attendants on the Inca.

As I have said, the rocks all over the plateau back of the Fortress, chiefly limestone, are cut and carved in a thousand forms. Here is a niche, or a series of them; anon a broad seat like a sofa, or a series of small seats; next a flight of steps; then a cluster of square, round, and octagonal basins; long lines of grooves; occasional holes drilled down to reservoirs in some fissure in the rock, widened artificially into a chamber—and all these cut with the accuracy and finish of the most skillful worker in marble. In one or two instances these rocks had walls of cut stones built up around or in part against them, and have traces of small edifices on their summits, conveying the impression that they were shrines, from within the hollowed chambers of which the wily priest uttered oracles in response to offerings of chicha or maize. One part of a low limestone cliff, not far from the Rodadero, is called the Chingana or "Labyrinth," and it well deserves the name. It is much fissured naturally. These fissures have been enlarged by art, and new passages opened, with low corridors, small apartments, niches, seats, etc., forming a maze in which it requires great care not to he entangled and lost. The interior and remoter ramifications can not now be followed, since General San Roman, when Prefect of Cuzco, had some of the passages walled up, in consequence of the recurrence of accidents—the last accident happening to three boys who were lost and starved to death in the recesses of the Chingana.

Niche in Terrace Walls of the Colcompata

There is a story current of two students who, many years ago, undertook the exploration of the Chingana, and followed its passage until they found themselves beneath the Temple of the Sun, and could distinctly hear the chanting of mass in the church of Santo Domingo, which occupies its site. "All of which," in the phrase with which committees end their reports, "is respectfully submitted."

I have thus described the great Fortress of the Sacsahuaman from the modern stand-point —as it is. It is a mistake of our old chronicler, Garcillaso, that the Fortress could not be commanded, not even by artillery. It is commanded in great part by the Rodadero at short musket-shot; and from the heights of Cantutpata, on the left of the rivulet Rodadero, it is completely commanded by the lightest artillery, and a portion of it by arrows. Still, it was no doubt an impregnable fortress, under the system of warfare practiced in ancient times, when slings and arrows were the longest-reaching of offensive arms.

The old authors differ as to the date of the construction of the Fortress of Cuzco. Garcillaso assigns it principally to Yupanqui, the tenth Inca, who came to power about the year 1400, and reigned thirty-nine years. He says that Pachacutic, ninth Inca, and father of Yupanqui, conceived the design, and left the plan with a great quantity of the stones prepared for building it; but that it was not finished until during the reign of Huayna Capac, the father of Atahualpa and Huascar, and but a short time before the arrival of the Spaniards.

Rock Seats, Near Fortress

Three hundred years have not sufficed to eradicate the notion that enormous treasures are concealed within the Fortress; nor have three hundred years of excavation, more or less constant, entirely discouraged the searchers for tapadas. In making our surveys of the work and of the Rodadero many were the eyes that watched us from behind rocks and stones, in full belief that the forasteros were there with some ancient itinerario obtained from Spain, determining by strange instruments the places where the Incas had hidden their wealth. More than once have we found, returning to our work in the mornings, the ground deeply excavated overnight where we had planted our little peg to determine the limit of our day's survey, and as a guide for resumption of our work. Often have I been approached by individuals of highest local position, with knowing and confidential hints and suggestions as to where the treasures were— merely as friends, to save us trouble, and with perfect willingness to make a fair division of the spoils; their traditional knowledge to offset our practical skill in treasure-hunting.

I doubt if, among all the people, high and low, whom I met in the Sierra, half a dozen could be found, when questioned apart, who would not testify to a belief that the investigation of ancient monuments was rather a clumsy pretext under which to carry on search for the chain of Huayna Capac or some other tapada of equal value, like the pexe grande of Chimu or the 10,000 llama loads of gold that were lost to the Spaniards by the premature execution of Atahualpa. And, if closely pressed, I think there are not a few who would take a distinct oath that my rather precipitate retreat to the coast, when the rains began to fall, was the immediate consequence of having been successful in my search. And I think it not impossible that the stones that were rolled down on us in the defiles of Andahuaylas were intended to create a confusion, wherein the mules laden with supposed Inca treasure could be stampeded, and the strangers and heretics spoiled. What a disappointment it would have been to the evil-minded assailants if they had succeeded in obtaining the coveted packages, only to find them filled with skulls and all uncleanness!

In a MS. in the British Museum, a copy of which is in my possession, I find recorded a curious story touching the supposed treasures of the Sacsahuaman, told by Felipe de Pomanes, who says:

"It is a well-known and acknowledged thing that in this Fortress of Cuzco there is a secret vault, in which is a vast treasure, since there were placed in it all the statues of the Incas, wrought in gold. And there is living today a lady who has been in this vault, named Doña Maria de Esquivel, wife of the last Inca, and whom I have heard describe how she came to go there, and what she saw there. It was thus: This lady had married Don Carlos Inca, who had not the means to keep up the state of the great personage that he really was, and the Doña Maria neglected him" [the chronicler says something worse], "because she had been deceived into marrying a poor Indian under the pretense that he was a great lord and Inca. And she so often repeated this reproach that Don Carlos one night said to her: 'Do you wish to know if I am the miserable pauper and wretch you accuse me of being? Do you wish to know if I am poor or rich? If so, come with me, and you shall see that I possess more wealth than any lord or king in the universe.' And Dona Maria, overcome by curiosity, consented to have her eyes bandaged—so unlike a woman—and to follow her indignant lord, who led her a number of turns, and then took her hand and conducted her down into a room, when he removed the bandage from her eyes, and she saw herself surrounded by unbounded treasures. In niches in the walls were many statues of all the Incas, as large as youths of twelve years old, all of finest gold, besides numberless vases of gold and silver, and blocks of the same, and altogether a wealth that convinced the lady that here was the grandest treasure of the world."

Coped and Niched Terrace Walls, Chinchero

How she behaved to her lord afterward the chronicler does not tell us; and whether she wheedled Don Carlos Inca out of a statue of his fathers, or a block of gold, we are unfortunately left in ignorance. But the chronicler does say that it is not to be presumed that an author of such judgment and character as Felipe de Pomanes would tell a story, even if it were possible that a lady of the character and known virtue of Dona Maria de Esquivel, could be guilty of such a thing.

All I can say is, that if the secret chamber that she entered has not yet been found and despoiled it has not been for default of digging, for I doubt if a foot of the soil of the Sacsahuaman has escaped being turned a dozen times over. Men were constantly busy there during the whole time of our stay. Perhaps our visit gave a new impulse to money-digging, or tapada-hunting, which, if called on to say, I should declare to be the principal occupation of the people of Peru. The time, labor, and money that have been spent in digging and dismantling ancient edifices, would have built a railway from one end of the country to the other—given wharves to the ports, and, what is far more needed, sewers to the cities

With this rapid notice of Cuzco and its Fortress I dismiss the Inca capital, with its numerous monuments and interesting traditions, and stride away to the famous Valley of Yucay, rich in soil, delightful in climate, luxuriant in vegetation, and varied in productions, where the Incas had their country seat, their baths, and their gardens. This valley, probably the most beautiful in Peru, is formed by the River Vilcanota, which we saw trickling from the dark tarn of La Raya, now swollen into a large stream, bearing the names, according to locality, of Vilcamayo, Urubamba, and Yucay. It is truly the Ucayali, and the parent stream of the Amazon. It is separated from the bolson of Cuzco by a high, irregular table land, or pupa, a hard day's journey across, although the distance in a right line can hardly exceed twenty miles. The Incas had two roads over this high bleak ridge; one leading direct from Cuzco to Yucay, with the intermediate establishment of Chinchero, where they had a palace; and the other more circuitous, by way of the plain of Chita, where the young Inca, Viracocha, chafed in exile, watching the flocks of his irate father, until the Brother of the Sun called him to victory and power. The roads, of which fragments remain, were formed of rough stones set in the ground, and were raised in the centre, with a row of larger stones set on edge on each side, through which at intervals there was an opening to pass off the water. The road was supported by terrace walls of cut stone in some places, where zig-zaging up declivities, evincing in plan and execution capable design and much skill.

In Chinchero are very elaborate remains. The present plaza of the town is an ancient square, flanked on one side by a terrace, supported by the most beautiful and elaborately niched retaining-wall that I saw in Peru, several hundred feet long. The structures, probably Inca palaces, built on this terrace have mainly disappeared, but a portion of the walls, corresponding with those of the Temple of the Sun in Cuzco, still form part of the vast and quaint church of the village. The ancient edifices stood back a little from the edge of the terrace, which is remarkable but by no means peculiar, in being crowned with a cornice or coping of large stones. The terrace is twelve feet high; most of the niches seven feet high by three feet ten inches wide at bottom, three feet ten inches at top, and two feet seven inches deep. Some years ago a portion of this fine terrace wall was torn down, and excavations made behind it by seekers for tapadas; and I must stop to applaud the deed of the then Prefect of the Department, Señor Guarmendia, who obliged the iconoclasts to replace the work they had destroyed. The restoration is shabby, for the wretches were unable to put together the stones they had torn apart—so much easier is it to destroy than to build up.

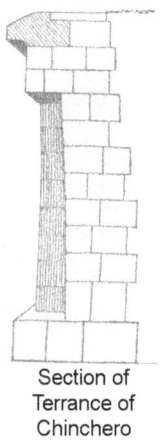

Section of
Terrance of
Chinchero

In the neighborhood of Chinchero are great sculptured rocks resembling those of the Sacsahuaman, if possible more elaborately cut and quite as enigmatical. The most interesting one is of limestone, cut in gradients, and with a bold projection like the pedestal of a statue, on which, sculptured in relief from the same rock, is the figure of a puma or tiger reclining on its side, with one of its young in its embrace as if suckling. The outline and action are well given, but the finer details are lost, inasmuch as it is the practice of the youth of the village to pelt with stones el gato de los gentiles, "the cat of the gentiles." The work probably suffered greatly from the hands of the early priests.

Two leagues beyond Chinchero we come to the abrupt edge of the table land on which it stands, and look almost sheer down on the Valley of Yucay, 4000 feet below. Here the traveler pauses instinctively, for the view before him is unsurpassed for beauty or grandeur by any on which his eyes have rested. In front rises that gigantic spur of the Andes which separates the valleys of the Vilcamayo and Paucurtambo, with rugged escarpments of bare rock, lofty snowy peaks and silvery glaciers, sharp, bright, and distinct, except when the clouds surge up its eastern side, to dissolve and disappear in flurries of snow on its summit. The great peaks of Chicon, Huacawasi, and Calca, tower up with a majesty scarcely second to that of the mighty Sorata, and with the abruptness of the Jungfrau, the Eigher, and the Matterhorn. The glaciers that lie between them have a sweep, as compared with those of the Alps, like that of a Western prairie as compared with a valley meadow of New England.

From the glittering crests of these vast mountains the eye ranges down, through every graduation of color and depth of shadow, past cleft and cliff, ravine and precipice, until it rests on the graceful andenes or terraces of the far-famed Gardens of Yucay. These sweep in curves around the feet of mountains, or project into the narrow valley through which steals the Rio Vilcamayo, in every combination of geometrical outline. Though now midwinter, and the crops are gathered in, yet the valley is gay with clumps of trees, gardens, and green hedgerows, which define the outlines of fields laid out by the Incas themselves, and with that regularity which distinguishes all the works of their hands. Although only about 2500 feet lower than the bolson of Cuzco, the Valley of Yucay, sheltered on every side, enjoys a climate much milder, corresponding very closely with that of

Nismes and the south of France. Equally salubrious and fertile, easily accessible from the capital, and with a vegetation exceptional in the Sierra, this sweet, calm valley, framed in by the loftiest mountains of the continent, became early the favorite resort of the Incas. Here they constructed those marvelous hanging gardens which, while they astonish by their extent and charm with their beauty, bear constant witness to the skill and the taste of their builders. Here, too, they built their palaces, and on every pass leading to their retreat they raised immense and impregnable fortresses. Borne hither in their golden palanquins, with a ceremony and pomp becoming the heads of a vast empire, surrounded by followers who revered them as embodying the power of the State and the majesty and sanctity of religion, the Incas must often have paused on the heights of Chinchero to gaze with awe and admiration on the grand panorama that here opened before them, and which the pencil may faintly portray but which the pen can not adequately describe. Before them the mighty mountain barriers they never could pass; at their feet the smiling valley of which their poets were never weary of singing, filled with the enduring works of their hands, and bright beneath the clear rays of the parent Sun. Under the inspiration of scenes like these, and in constant contact with Nature in her grandest forms, it would have been wonderful indeed if the Incas had not risen to conceptions higher and ideas more expanded than the dwellers in the gloom of the dense forests and among the jungles of the Amazon, where the sun only penetrates to quicken deadly vapors, and where life is a vain warfare against an unconquerable vegetation, fierce animals, venomous reptiles, and insects scarcely less poisonous.

The descent from the altos of Chinchero into the valley is long, laborious, and dangerous. Fragments of the zig-zag road of the Incas still remain, supported by heavy walls of masonry, broad enough for six persons to pass abreast, and of easy gradients. Although its careful preservation would seem to have been dictated by the commonest prudence, for there are few points where the escarpment of the plateau can be overcome, yet this artfully constructed road has been allowed to fall into utter ruin by the wretched successors of the provident Incas.

What at once arrests the attention of the visitor to the Valley of Yucay is the vast system of terraces that lines it on both sides, wherever the conformation of the ground admits of their construction, and of which the so-called andenes or gardens of the Inca, form part. These terraces, rising from the broader ones at the edge of the level grounds, climb the circumscribing mountains to the height of from 1000 to 1500 feet, narrowing as they rise, until the topmost ones are scarcely two feet broad. The terrace walls are of rough stones, well laid, slightly inclining inward, and of varying height of from three to fifteen feet. Very often an azequia or artificial aqueduct, starting high up some narrow ravine, at the very verge of the snow, is carried along the mountain sides, above or through the andenes, from which water is taken for irrigation—running from one terrace to the next, and carefully distributed over all. Access from one terrace to another is variously effected; sometimes by zig-zag paths; sometimes by regular stairs; but oftenest through the device to which I have had occasion to refer, of projecting stones. This description will apply to the ordinary mountain terraces, of which the whole country is full, and which were built to retain the earth on the steep mountain and hillsides, which would otherwise be washed away.

But the more elaborate andenes are those built as are those of Yucay, the most extensive, most regular, and most beautiful of all Peru. They are raised at the mouth of a gorge, which has a rapid fall from among the splintered summits of the Nevada of Calca, and which enters the valley at its widest part, and nearly at right angles to it. Through this leaps out from the rocky entrance to the mountains a bright, clear stream, fed from the drip of the impending glaciers and snowy peaks, which, in the course of ages, has brought down a great mass of debris, rock, and earth, that, until smoothed down and made symmetrical by the Incas, must have been a rude and disfiguring heap in the valley. The first step seems to have been to confine the stream in a single channel, between walls of stone; next to construct a series of semicircular terraces, supported by rude but durable walls, over which the stream leaps in a series of cataracts. As the declivity lessens these terraces become broader, and the stream is diverted into several channels, each feeding a new series of terraces, falling off in front and flank of the central one in almost every possible combination in outline of the square and the circle—in gradients, like the pyramids, and so artfully that the water from the stream is evenly distributed over them all and then carried off to irrigate the wide wings that sweep in grand lines of beauty around the bases of the mountains up and down the valley. The central and most elevated series of terraces, which pushes out boldly in the plain, is made up chiefly of square areas, with flanking aprons, filled with richest soil, from which the stones have all been carefully removed, and which nurtures that noblest of native cereals, the maize blanca, or white maize of Yucay. Upon one of these areas, with broad terraces on every side or circling away in graceful perspective, with the white glaciers of Calca impending behind, and the mural face of the Plateau of Chinchero rising in front—high up among the andenes, where the eye commands long reaches of teeming valley and of the river with its burnished pools and swirling rapids, surrounded by lofty pisote trees clothed in unfading green and glowing like sunset with their orange-colored flowers, amidst baths and fountains and the murmur of falling waters—stood the Summer Palace of the Incas. Only a few sad remnants attest its site and signify its finished architecture. The delicately-cut stones of which it was built went early to construct the churches of the neighboring villages of Huaylabamba, Calca, Urquillos, Urubamba, and the convents that the warrior priests of the Conquest were not slow to raise in the genial and fertile valley of Yucay.

I commenced my explorations in the valley from the town of Urubamba—"Plain of the Spider"—the capital of the district, which is entered over a lofty stone bridge of ninety feet span, and between two rows of gigantic willows. The town itself is like all other towns of the Sierra, but its position can hardly be surpassed in beauty—a beauty enhanced, to our eyes, by the reappearance of a verdure to which we had long been strangers. Apart from great willows and gigantic pisotes, we found other familiar varieties of trees. Hundreds of wild cherry-trees lined the roads, some in blossom and some in fruit, while peaches and apples, oranges and lemons, hung temptingly in the gardens.

Our host, Señor Umeres, was the Sub-Prefect of the district, a very enterprising, and, for the country, a very intelligent man, who provided us with mules for our visit to Ollantaytambo, and a letter of recommendation to the Gobernador of that frontier town, lying eight leagues distant, down the valley of the river.

The ride to this point is extremely varied and interesting, amidst scenery alternately grand and picturesque. At a distance of three leagues, the road running between stone-walls and rows of cherry and peach trees, and lined with rude stone-houses, we came to where a broad gorge opened between lofty mountains on our right. This gorge extends high up into a region of mist and snow, to a great glacier, or a series of glaciers, which appear to unite in it from different directions. A very considerable stream emerges from these, which, however, distributes itself into several channels over a vast mass of rocks and stones and gravel, with scrubby bushes interspersed, that has been swept or crowded down through the gorge, filling up the valley for miles, and pressing close on the river, where, owing to the wash of the stream, it presents a perpendicular face of indurated material at least two hundred feet high, cut into fantastic, castellated forms, like an aggregation of old Gothic cathedrals. To descend this escarpment was no easy matter, the path being both narrow and precipitous and full of rolling stones; and when once down the road was a ticklish one, between cliff and river. Further on, beyond this mass of debris, the valley widens out into a sort of marshy pampa, on the further edge of which we discerned an ancient Inca edifice, connected with a series of extensive terraces and other complicated works, too much ruined to be intelligible. Immediately back of the structure, however, rises a high cliff, the face of which is full of ancient tombs; that is to say, of excavations natural and artificial in the rock, within which the dead were placed, and then walled up with stones, stuccoed over, and painted. Many of these seemed absolutely inaccessible, or to be reached only by ropes let down from above. We contrived, however, to clamber up to several of them, from which I obtained several interesting skulls. The fronts of some of the least protected tombs had fallen away, and the bones of their former inmates were scattered at the foot of the cliff, or lay in full view on the narrow shelves of rock.

Beyond this Golgotha the valley narrows again between bare

cliffs from two to three thousand feet high, leaving just room enough for the roadway and river—the latter deep and swift and of a bright green color. Our view was limited to a strip of blue sky above, and to the snowy mountain of Chicon, which rose white and sepulchral directly in front, as if blocking up the valley and prohibiting further passage. Again the valley widened, and we rode through a forest of Spanish broom, which here becomes really arborescent, covered thickly with brilliantly-yellow and oppressively-fragrant flowers, among which darted a great variety of hummingbirds, some of them as large as swallows. The mountains now fall further back from the river, it becomes less rapid, and on the opposite or left bank the ground spreads out in broad meadows and cultivated grounds.

Descending through these, at right angles to the river, from a dark and rugged gorge, we noticed a considerable stream, the Rio Guarconda, draining the high bolson or Valley of Antis. There is a rough and dangerous pathway through this gorge to the plain above, which the Incas protected by works of considerable extent at its mouth. But their principal works were built further down the stream, at a point where a low ridge extends nearly across the valley. This ridge had been terraced up with high, vertical walls, rising from the very bed of the stream, on every side, to the height of nearly one hundred feet. Held by any considerable body of men, it commanded completely the passage of the valley. The river pours with arrow-like rapidity between these terraces and the rocky escarpment opposite, along the face of which runs the narrow and dizzy pathway over which all travelers to Ollantaytambo are obliged to pass.

From this point forward for a league the valley is narrowed to a mere cleft between mountains rising in rugged masses, but with almost vertical fronts, to enormous elevations. The brain reels in straining to discern their splintered summits. Dark and chill, this is one of the grand portadas or mountain gateways of the Andes leading to the plains of the Amazon, of which the early chroniclers write with undissembled awe. The river looks black and sinister in the subdued light, and its murmur subsides into a hollow roar. The shrubs of broom become scant and small, and their flowers are few and mean. In front rises forever the white, ghastly Chicon. We hasten through this gloomy gorge as fast as our mules can travel, and rejoice when the valley again commences to spread out, and we can see patches of sunlight in the open space that invites us onward. Still the river presses us close to the mountain, at the base of which is a series of narrow, ruined andenes, while on the opposite bank of the river, again confined between heavy artificial walls, we notice a long building of two stories, with turrets and loop-holes, hanging against the mountain, and dominating a narrow pathway that runs between it and the rapid, compressed river. It more resembles the castles of the Rhine and the Lower Rhone than any thing we have yet seen, and would be regarded as a most striking and picturesque object in any part of the world.

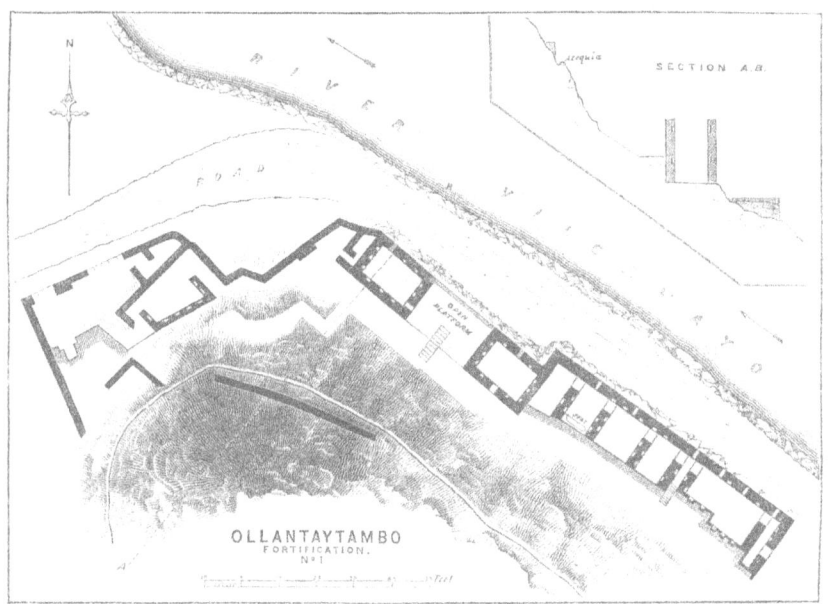

OLLANTAYTAMBO
FORTIFICATION.
N° 1

A little further the mountains on our right send out a high spur of bare rock directly in front and across our path, deflecting the river across the valley, which now widens out in broad and beautiful intervals, as level as a table, in which we discover men and oxen plowing. At the extremity of this rocky barrier, and between it and the wall against which the river frets and swirls, is a narrow roadway, overshadowed by the Cyclopean walls of another fortress or outwork, above which, perched on the cliffs, at every elevation, we see round towers of stone of varying sizes, with port holes opening on our line of approach, and from which stones might be precipitated on our very heads. The roadway is partially blocked with the debris of one of these towers and many tons of the rock on which it once stood, all of which had fallen down during the heavy rains of the preceding summer. These rock-slips are frequent among the Andes, sometimes rendering the so-called roads impassable, and occasionally damming up the rivers, when the water, setting back, will form deep, narrow lakes until it breaks through all obstructions in a devastating flood below.

Passing around this salient outwork, our path ascends a series of terraces, underneath niched and crenated walls, until the upper terrace is reached, on which the road runs. An ancient azequia is high above on the rock's side, in which we hear the gurgle of invisible waters. Here, still clinging to the foot of the mountains, we look down past the andenes on level fields, which in the proper season must support a wealth of grain. But directly in front, extending as before transversely across the valleys and at right angles to our path, their edges defined by tall willows and flowering shrubs, with water leaping brightly in mimic cataracts from one to the other, we discover the famous terraces of Ollantaytambo. Standing on the edge of the topmost, in strong relief, is a group of buildings which our guide points out as the house of the Governor of Ollantaytambo, to whom we are recommended. It was getting late; we were hungry certainly, and tired withal; and we spurred our mules forward toward our resting-place. Soon we came to a massive crenated wall, pierced by two gateways with grooves in their piers, as if to receive a sliding portcullis, and flanked on the beetling ledges of the mountain by round loop-holed towers, like those already mentioned. Beyond, the road led between two ancient stone buildings, still inhabited, which fill the space between the edge of the terrace and the cliffs, apparently designed as guardhouses, and between which the visitor to Ollantaytambo had to pass in the olden, as he has to do in the modern time. Past these the road continues between a high niched wall on one hand, and the cliff with its gurgling azequia on the other. Thus shut in 'twixt wall and mountain, and our view circumscribed, we jog on for half a mile. Then the wall ends. A lane leads off to our left at right angles for a few hundred yards between stone-walls and hedges of flowering shrubs, when we come to a sort of shrine, in which is a crumbling cross covered with faded ribbons and withered flowers. Here we turn again, and again at right angles, and at the end of another long lane, with an azequia running through its centre, we discover the house or group of houses belonging to the Gobernador. They are low and mean enough in reality, but in the purple shadow of the mountains, over whose tops the setting sun casts a crimson glow, they look a blissful haven of rest. Our mules pricked up their ears, and with visions of infinite alfalfa before them broke into a lively trot, carrying us through the gateway and into the paved court of the Gobernador's house with a spirited clang and clatter that made us feel that we were caballeros if not conquerors.

The Gobernador was a man of wealth as well as of consequence, hospitable, and reasonably intelligent. His house is built around a court, in which the horses are tethered, the cattle fed, the pigs allowed to roam without restraint, in company with the dogs, the geese, the ducks, the chickens, and the little cues or indigenous guinea-pigs that go squeaking in and out every crevice in the walls. For the delectation of all of these the azequia runs through the centre of the court into a paved pool, whence it is conducted over the terraces to help irrigate the level lands below. From this pool the cattle drink; in it the pigs wallow, and the geese and ducks disport themselves. From it the water you drink and wash in is ladled up; in it the dishes you ate from are cleansed; and if, when the modest night drops its curtain, you peep through the cracks of your door you may discern the servants of the establishment bathing in it. Not too often, however. But the water flows in rapidly at one extremity, and is discharged with equal rapidity at the other, and you take it for granted it carries all impurities with it.

Señor Benavente gave us an apartment about twelve feet square next to the close den in which the servants slept. It had the advantage of a small unglazed window under the eaves, and a door which would shut, requiring only to be braced with a stick from the inside. Dinner he served us in his own sala, which had a mud floor, an unsteady table, and a long bench whereon to sit. There was a hide bed in the corner, with saddles and bridles draped over it, improvised, the Gobernador said, because the Señora his wife, whose suppressed moans we could hear through a thin partition of cotton cloth, was ill of fever. I administered, after due solicitation: blue pills, two at night; grains of quinine fifteen in the morning; chicken broth, light, in the interval. To be repeated daily. Cure complete in three days.

We had some difficulty in disposing our mattresses in our narrow quarters, when the Gobernador came and shared our coffee and cognac.

I inquired minutely about the antiquities, the Fortress, the Tarpeian Rock, the great "Tired Stones," the quarries, the Inca Bridge, and about all the marvelous things we had been told existed here, and about all of which el Gobernador was much confused, and, as we thought, very ignorant. Finally, wearied by my questions, he said he had a book which explained everything concerning "los Reyes Incas," which he would fetch. He did so. It was a translation of Prescott's Peru.

We were up and out early; and, although a little chill the morning was clear and glorious. Not a ray of sunlight fell in the valley, but the clouds that clung to the summits of the high mountains rising on either hand were a mass of gold and crimson. No light, however, seemed to touch the giant bulk of Chicon, that still rose before us, as calm and pale as death, and as remote as ever. The mountains on all sides, as I have said, are steep, even precipitous, but yet we discerned at elevations of thousands of feet on their rocky flanks, where it seemed that only the condor could reach, large and regular edifices! One in particular appeared to impend over the Gobernador's rude but hospitable dwelling. It had never been visited, the Gobernador said, by human being in modern times, whereupon Mr. C— made a vow that he would climb up to it, and measure it withal; which he did, to the amazement not of the Gobernador alone, but of all the chocolate-colored denizens of Ollantaytambo.

Between coffee and breakfast-time we were conducted past long reaches of terrace walls, and through the village of Ollantaytambo which in plan and structure is little changed from what it was under Inca rule—across a turbulent, icy, glacier-fed stream, milky in color from the ground rock held in suspension, which descends from the transverse ravine of Patacancha to the Fortress—a work less imposing than that of the Sacsahuaman, but more complicated and with equal evidence of skill. I went there often during our stay of two weeks in Ollantaytambo, surveyed it carefully, and made drawings and photographs of its more important features. It is built on the spur of a great snowy mountain that projects between the two valleys of Patacancha and the river of which I have so often spoken, each side of which, except where it presents a sheer escarpment of rock, is built up with terraces, ascended on one side by steps, and on the other by an inclined plane over half a mile long. This plane, up which the gigantic stones for the Fortress had been moved, and on which many of them still rest, is protected at intervals by square buildings of stone, looped, something like our blockhouses, and is supported by a wall of stones, inclining inward, and in places upward of sixty feet high.

Doorway to Corridor, Ollantaytambo.

The exterior walls of the Fortress zig-zag up the mountain side, and turning at right angles, extend to where a precipice, more than a thousand feet high, makes their prolongation impossible and unnecessary. They are about twenty-five feet high, built of rough stones stuccoed outside and inside, crenated, and have an inner shelf for the convenience of defenders. They might easily be mistaken for the work of Robert Guiscard, and are not unlike the Middle-Age fortifications of that chief that hang on the brow of the hills above Salerno in Italy.

Within the walls, and on the projecting rocky point which they isolate from the mountain, is a confused mass of buildings and walls, great porphyritic blocks, closely fitted in place or lying isolated, rock-cut seats, doorways of beautifully hewn stones with jambs inclining inward, long ranges of niches in Cyclopean walls, stairways and terraces, with a shabby and tottering wooden cross at the extremity of all, bending over the village which lies like a map beneath.

It would require far more space than I can afford to properly describe the Fortress, nor would a description be intelligible without the aid of plans and sections. The stones composing it, or lying scattered over its area, are of a hard red porphyry, brought from quarries more than two leagues distant, upward of three thousand feet above the valley, and on the opposite side from the Fortress. They are nearly all hewn into shape and ready to be fitted, and among them I noticed several having places cut in them for the reception of the T clamp, which I have mentioned in describing the remains of Tiahuanaco. One of these porphyry blocks, built in the wall of what appeared to be the beginning of a square building, is eighteen feet long by five broad and four deep, not only perfectly squared but finely polished on every face, as are also the stones adjoining it, to which it fits with scarcely perceptible joints.

The most interesting series of stones, however, are six great upright slabs of porphyry supporting a terrace, against which they slightly incline. The engraving will illustrate their character better than any description. It will be observed that they stand a little apart, and that the spaces between them are accurately filled in with other thin stones, in sections. The sides of these, as well as of the larger slabs which they adjoin, are polished.

The following table gives the dimensions of the slabs in feet and tenths, commencing with the one at the left:

	No. 1.	No. 2.	No. 3.	No. 4.	No. 5.	No. 6.
Height	11.5	10.7	12.8	12.1	12.4	13.5
Width at base..	6.2	4.7	3.7	5.7	7.0	7.1
Width at top...	5.4	4.4	4.2	6.0	6.8	6.4
Thickness......	4.0	3.5	2.3	2.6	2.5	5.9

It will be seen that the faces of these slabs are not hewn entirely smooth, but have several projections, indicating that the work of accurately facing them was never completed. Number 4 shows traces of the same kind of ornamentation observed on some of the blocks at Tiahuanaco, only here the ornament is in relief.

But gigantic as are these blocks, they are small in comparison with the "Tired Stones" lying on the inclined plane leading to the Fortress or at its foot, as if abandoned there by the ancient workmen. One of these is twenty-one feet six inches long, by fifteen feet broad. It is partly imbedded in the ground, but shows a thickness of five feet above the soil.

The view from the Fortress in every direction is wonderful in variety, in contrast, in beauty and grandeur. The whole valley of Ollantaytambo is laid out like a garden, in a system of terraces, one below the other, falling off step by step to the river, each terrace level as a billiard table, or with just enough of declivity to permit of easy irrigation. The river flows at the very feet of the bare majestic mountains on its further side, and falling into it at right angles is the chafing, turbulent, mountain, snow-fed torrent, to which I have alluded, descending from the steep valley or gorge of Patacaucha or Marca-cocha, in which rise, one above another, a long vista of green terraces like the seats in a Roman amphitheatre. The portada, through which we entered this wonderful vale, looks dark and forbidding, and the turreted fortress that defends it appears stern and threatening under the shadow of the mountains that close in around it. Looking down the valley, there stands always the death-white, silent Chicon, apparently barring all passage, and repelling all approach. Facing us, most remarkable and impressive of all, is the Mountain of Pinculluna, or "Hill of Flutes," an abrupt, splintered mass of rock, thousands of feet high, cutting the sky sharply with its jagged crest. Hanging against its sides, in positions apparently, and in some places really, inaccessible, are numerous buildings. One group—a series of five long edifices, one above the other, on corresponding narrow terraces—is the "School of the Virgins." On a bold, projecting rock, with a vertical descent of upward of 900 feet, stands a small building, with a doorway opening on the very edge of the precipice; it is the "Horca del Hombre," the Tarpeian rock of Ollantaytambo, over which male criminals were thrown, in the severe Draconian days of the Incas. Above it, at a little distance, on a narrow shelf, are the prisons in which the criminals awaited their doom. To the left of these again, separated by a great chasm in the mountain, but at the same giddy height, and overlooking another precipice not less appalling, is the "Horca de Muger," or place of execution for women—vestals false to their vows, or ñustas faithless to their Inca lords. These airy spots I subsequently visited, obtaining drawings and plans of them all—too voluminous by far for these pages.

Porphyry Slabs, Fortress of Ollantaytambo

I have said that the village of Ollantaytambo is little changed from Inca times. The old central square of the town, the Manay-racay, or "Court of Petitions," is nearly perfect, and one of the Inca buildings, near it and at the feet of the precipices of the Fortress, is completely so, lacking only the roof. It is a story and a half high, built of rough stones laid in clay, and originally stuccoed, with a solid central wall reaching to the apex of the gables, dividing it into two apartments of equal size. The corners of the building, the jambs, and lintels of the lower doors are of cut stones. There seems to have been no access to the upper story from the interior, but there are two entrances to it through one of the gables, where four flat, projecting stones seem to have supported a kind of balcony or platform, reached probably by ladders.

Nothing can exceed the regularity and taste with which the ancient town was laid out, the streets running parallel to the stream that watered it, which was, and is, confined between walls of stone. Regular terraces of richest soil, with flights of steps at intervals, rise from the stream to the level terreplein on which the town stands, and which extends back to the cliffs of the Pinculluna. The longitudinal streets are about fourteen feet broad; the transverse ones nine feet. Each block is surrounded by a high wall, itself forming part of the walls of a double series of buildings, as shown in the plan; and each series has a central court and three dependent ones. What may be called the central or principal building, facing the entrances, is half in one group and half in the other, divided longitudinally by a wall continued up to the apex of the gables. Like the building just described, the upper half story was entered through a door in the gable, the sill of which was a broad, flat projecting stone, reached by series of flat stones set, stairwise, in the wall dividing the two groups of buildings forming the "block."

These ancient houses, substantially perfect, are still inhabited, and in their arrangement and other respects give us an accurate notion of the mode in which the ancients lived. We detect a rigid system and order such as might be supposed to exist in a Fourier establishment, or a penitentiary, and suggesting a probable division and subdivision of the people into ranks and orders. Of course the long, dull lines of walls, with no other openings than a single, heavily-jambed doorway in each block, give the cramped streets a gloomy, monotonous appearance, and the eye turns from them with a sense of relief to the bright sky above, and to the lofty, splintered, and snowy mountains that terminate the view in every direction through their narrow vistas.

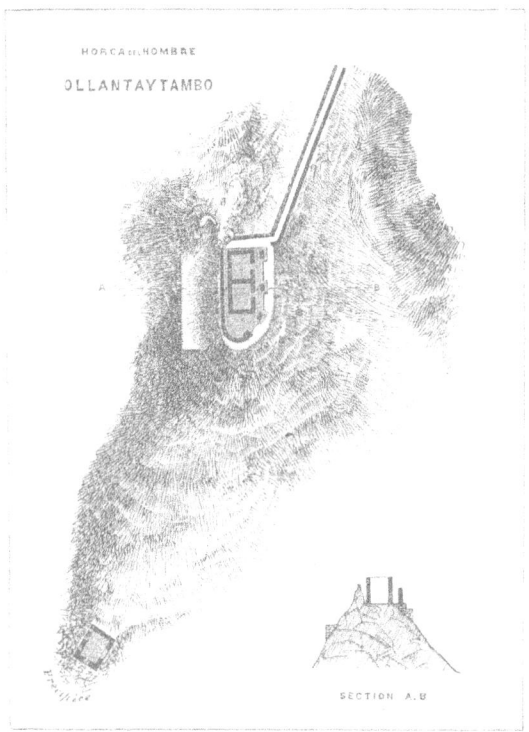

If the town of Ollantaytambo is substantially what it was four hundred years ago, so, too, are the inhabitants—of whom none that I encountered spoke any language except the Quichua. They are a quiet, saturnine, and industrious people, not specially addicted to the Catholic religion, I should think, in view of the ruinous condition of their little church; although I must give them the credit of having followed my photographic boxes through the plaza with uncovered heads, kissing them devoutly, under the mistaken notion that they contained reliques of the saints.

A few days after our arrival the Governor arranged to conduct us to the great porphyry quarries of the ancients, high up on the shoulders of the mountains on the other side of the river, at the foot of a lofty and impressive peak, almost always enveloped in clouds. We crossed the river on a bridge of mimbres or braided withes —a suspension bridge, in fact, but of the rudest description—a perpetuation of those in universal use at the time of the Conquest. There are thousands of such bridges to this day in Peru. This particular bridge is distinguished as being in two spans, of about 40 feet each, reaching from the opposite shores of the river to a pier of heavy stones, of unmistakable Inca workmanship, in the centre of the stream. A great rock lies just above the pier, which tradition affirms was placed there for its protection against the force of the current; but we thought more likely that this natural protection suggested the feasibility of erecting the pier, which would have to be massive indeed to resist the rush of the Vilcamayo at certain seasons. As I have said, the bridge consists of several great cables of braided withes or branches, chiefly of a tough kind of shrub called ioke, placed side by side and firmly anchored by a variety of clumsy devices to buttresses on the banks of the river. Sticks are placed transversely across these, and fastened to the cables with thongs of rawhide or with vines, forming a roadway about four feet wide. Above this rude roadway, and less for support of the bridge than as a protection against falling off the yielding, swaying, and apparently unstable structure, are two smaller cables, elevated a few feet, one on each side, with vines or cords reaching down to the bridge at intervals, forming a kind of netting, but so far apart as to afford slight security against danger. Not long before our visit a drunken Indian and his wife and mule stumbled from the bridge and were lost. Mr. D—, however, rode his horse across with the utmost nonchalance. These bridges are seldom level, and, besides sagging greatly, often get "lopsided," when, in wet weather, the sticks corresponding to plankings become so slippery that it is no easy matter to retain one's footing. There is another and greater danger in passing the long bridges of this kind, like the famous ones over the river Apurimac and Pampas; namely, their swaying to and fro like hammocks when the wind sweeps through the deep gorges, across which they are suspended at heights so great that they appear as light and airy as cobwebs. It often happens that they become impassable, and that travelers are detained for days from this cause.

Past the bridge of Ollantaytambo, our road ran along a narrow shelf between the foot of the desolate mountain and the river; here partly cut in the rock, and yonder supported by a retaining wall built up from the edge of the water. Indeed the river throughout, except where a sheer precipice closes in on it from one side or the other, is confined between ancient artificial walls of such excellent workmanship that its impetuous waters have failed to dislodge them in the lapse of centuries. Nothing could be more beautiful than the system of terraces supporting the rich, level fields and meadows of Ollantaytambo on the opposite bank. They bend in and out with the sinuosities of the river, in graceful curves, their stony faces relieved by the vines and shrubs that cling up against them or droop in festoons over their edges. No visitor can see them without being amazed at the skill, patience, and power to which they bear, and will bear for ages, a silent but impressive testimony.

Inca Building, Ollantaytambo

At the distance of half a league a high, rocky spur of the mountain projected itself boldly before us, presenting a vertical front to the river. Around its feet the waters swirled and fretted in impotent rage. The path over it is narrow; so narrow that two animals can not pass each other, besides being steep and stony. On the summit itself stand two towers, flanked by an impassable rock toward the river, little smaller than those that crown the headlands of the Mediterranean, with openings like port-holes to complete the resemblance. The way lies between them, in a deep notch in the rock, through which a loaded mule can barely pass. At the base of the towers, on the other side, we noticed the remains of buildings, the quarters probably of the garrison that held this almost impregnable position in the days of yore.

Further on, the mountain slope is less abrupt, and its face is terraced up for many hundreds of feet, to a comparatively broad shelf on the mountain side, where are the remains of an ancient village. We ascend through these andens, by a steep, rough path, to a headland also dominating the river in front. The path is narrow enough to flutter most nerves, and a false step would send man and mule whirling into the rocky bed of the river brawling, now almost inaudibly, below. Clambering over the headland, we descended rapidly to a broad and beautiful road, with gentle grade, winding along the flank of the ridge, and reaching far back toward the head of a mighty ravine intervening between the buttress on which we stand, and another, equally bold, a mile or two distant. This is the old Inca road leading to the porphyry quarries whence the giant stones of the Fortress of Ollantaytambo were obtained. We follow this to the very extremity and brow of the headland, over which they were toppled, sliding down two thousand feet into the valley. The plane worn in their descent is distinct, and lying around us are blocks more or less shaped artificially, which the apparition of the Spaniards prevented the ancient workmen from launching down to their destination. How these blocks were got across the swift and turbulent river, in the bed of which some still remain, I do not attempt to explain.

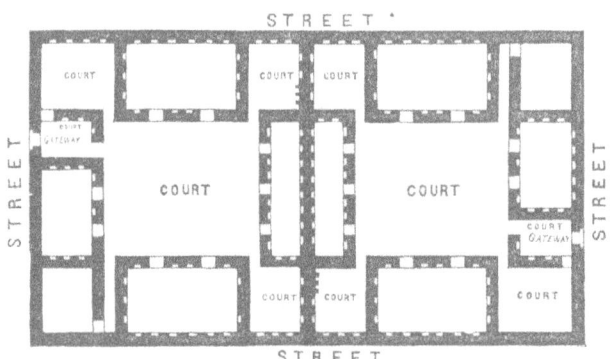

An Ancient Block in Ollantaytambo

Starting back along the ancient quarry road we constantly

encountered blocks of porphyry, entirely or partly hewn, some in the middle of the road, and others lying by its sides. Traces of rude cottages, and evidences of attempts at cultivation in little areas between the rocks, are visible at intervals.

Two miles of this, and we see rising before us and extending across the head of the ravine two vast walls of stone, more than a fourth of a mile long, and from thirty to fifty feet high—the retaining walls of terraces designed to receive the great rocks that man, or time, or the earthquakes, may wrench or splinter off from the impending porphyry cliffs, and prevent their tearing down the steep declivity of the ravine into the valley, where, apparently at our very feet, we discern the tile roofs and clustering huts of the richest hacienda of Ollantaytambo. Piled on the terraces supported by these massive walls, which incline inward toward the mountain to secure greater strength, are confused masses of porphyry blocks, thousands on thousands, as if a glacier had been converted into stone. Some of these, in their descent, have torn away portions of the retaining-walls designed to stay their headlong course. A few have passed both barriers, and are heaped below the lowest in threatening readiness to take a final plunge into the smiling vale three thousand feet below.

Perched on some of the largest of these rocks are dozens of little buildings, somewhat resembling the chulpas of the Collao, but scarcely bigger than the toy-houses that children build. They are of rough stones laid in clay, and roofed, or rather arched, with other flat stones overlapping each other like the tiles of modern dwellings, and projecting over the walls so as to form a rude cornice. Some of these curious structures are square, but most of them are round, from four to five feet high, with about the same diameter, and all have little doorways, opening, for the most part, toward the ragged, threatening cliffs. A few show traces of having been stuccoed and painted inside. Our first impression was that they were the tombs of the ancient quarrymen; but we found no human bones in any of them, and finally came to the conclusion that they were shrines, like those around Vesuvius. But instead of containing a figure of St. Januarius or other saint, had held some huaca or sacred object, placed there to arrest the danger of the mighty rock avalanches that had piled up their porphyritic masses in a ragged wilderness above and around them.

Most of the ancient stone-cutting had been done on the lower terrace, as evinced by heaps of chippings on every side. Here the ancient road ends.

Our host insisted that the real quarry was some hundreds of feet higher up. To reach the spot we had to climb a lateral ridge that no one but a traveler among the Andes would dream of being accessible, and up which we scrambled with infinite labor and no little risk. The summit of the ridge presented quite a broad area, in great part covered with porphyritic rocks heaped up in the same dire confusion that I have already described, at the foot of a bare peak, of the same material, from which they had splintered off, and which presented toward us an absolutely precipitous face. The point where we stood was 3240 feet above the valley, and this rocky warder must tower up to treble that height. I have said that its summit is usually lost in clouds; but this day it stood out sharp and clear against the sky, revealing all its rugged features. A few condors were circling in front of it and around its lofty head, the only things of life to be seen. Yet here the patient, persevering Incas had cleared the cold soil of stones, and built up little andenes, to gain scant areas for the hardy mountain grasses on which the llamas feed.

We found no wrought stones here, but many which appeared to have been split into regular blocks, chiefly parallelopipeds, of varying dimensions. The greater number were from eight inches to a foot square at the ends, and from six to ten feet long; but there were others much longer, and which, tradition insists, were intended to be girders for the bridge which we had passed in the morning. I measured one of these, and found it to be twenty feet six inches long, by two feet one inch broad, and one foot nine inches thick. I can hardly believe that these were produced by natural cleavage; yet, as before said, there are no traces of tools on them.

Our descent to the valley was rapid enough, but not composing to the nerves. At the hacienda we found the cura of the village, who had just returned from Cuzco, and was anxiously awaiting "los Franceses." All foreigners in the Sierra are supposed by the mixed population to be French by nationality, and peddlers of jewelry by occupation. He advised us not to go down the valley to Santa Ana, adding, significantly, that the peones there had ascertained the real value of the glittering wares that the last Franceses had disposed of there. And then he wanted to see what trinkets we had with us, and intimated the possibility of making a purchase. It was with difficulty that I convinced him that we were not peddlers, when he inquired, what, in the name of the Santissamo Trinidad, had brought us to Ollantaytambo? "Antiquidades!" he repeated after me, with unfeigned astonishment, became suddenly silent, and left the room. Directly he returned to the door and beckoned me to come out to a remote corner of the court among the horses. Like the cura of Tiahuanaco, he, too, was weary of life in an Indian village; he knew the soil was stuffed with treasure, and understood perfectly the object of our visit. It was well enough to disguise it from the people generally and the Gobernador in particular; but now we might just as well take him into our confidence and divide the spoils we had come so far to obtain. Like the cura of Tiahuanaco —and, for that matter, nearly all the curas in the Sierra—he was maudlin, and wept. I respected his tears, and thinking from my silence that my heart was touched and the seals of my confidence melted, he became finally composed; and then I shocked him by insisting that "antiguidades," and only "antiguidades," had brought us to Ollantaytambo. This was too much; the face of the Lord's minister became livid under the starlight, and he strode away with the ominous suggestion, "All the roads are bad that lead from Ollantaytambo!"

I described our interview to the Gobernador, who did not seem to regard it as a laughing matter, and was not at all reassuring when he said that the cura was a great scoundrel, and quite capable of attempting harm. It was good for that cura that we did not meet him in any of the narrow passes on our road back to Urubamba, for we very likely would have shot him before inquiring the reason of his being there.

After what I have said and intimated in these papers about the priesthood in Peru, it is perhaps supererogatory to add a paragraph concerning them from the "Apuntes y Observeclones" of Don Juan Bustamente, a native and resident of the Sierra. "It is sixty years," says Don Juan, "since the Department of Puno has seen a Bishop, and as a consequence of this strange abandonment, the curas live according to their fancies, gratifying their passions without restraint or fear of any kind, carrying their scandals to the extent of living publicly with their concubines and bastards." The reason assigned by Don Juan for the demoralization of the clergy of Puno certainly can not apply in the Department of Cuzco, where there have been bishops enough, but where about the same lax condition of things prevails that he so loudly deplores.

No portion of my stay in Peru was more pleasant or profitable than that passed in Ollantaytambo. It was in the season called winter, and the winds that swept through the valley were fierce, yet most of the trees retained their foliage, and the bushes along the azequias were green and blooming with flowers, among which toyed at morn and eventide such numbers of humming-birds as I have rarely seen, even in the tangled thickets of Nicaragua, where prolific Nature exhausts her energies in swelling the sum of animal and vegetable life. Doves and pigeons of many kinds cooed among the branches, and little cues skurried along the terrace walls, or in a tame condition nestled around our feet, inspiring constant fear that an unlucky step might crush out their innocent and busy lives. On every hand were traces and monuments of ancient art, industry, and intelligence. Enigmatical buildings, towers, and terraces impended on the mountain sides; fortresses in positions skillfully selected, and themselves artfully designed closed every approach, and frowned from every direction while in the centre, overhanging the ancient town, rose the stately citadel. In the valley Art had leveled every inequality, and raised hundreds of miles of terraces, filled with earth scraped from hill slopes and mountain side, and watered by azequias whose channels were carried along the faces of inaccessible cliffs, or tunneled through rocky projections which it was impossible to turn. And high over all, a square building, in which was the Intihuatana or Gnomon of the Sun, by means of which the solstices and equinoxes, the seasons of planting and harvests, and the periods of the great festivals were determined and their arrival proclaimed.

Ollantaytambo was the frontier town and Fortress of the Incas in the Valley of the Ucayale, as it is today of their conquerors. There were outlying works some leagues lower down the river at

Havaspampa, but the bulwark of the empire against the savage Antis in this direction was here. It is around Ollantaytambo also that cling the traditions of Ollantay, the lovelorn chieftain, whose thwarted affections drove him into rebellion against the Vicegerent of the Sun, and whose suffering and adventures form the basis of the nearest perfect and the best of all the dramas of Ancient America that have descended to our days.

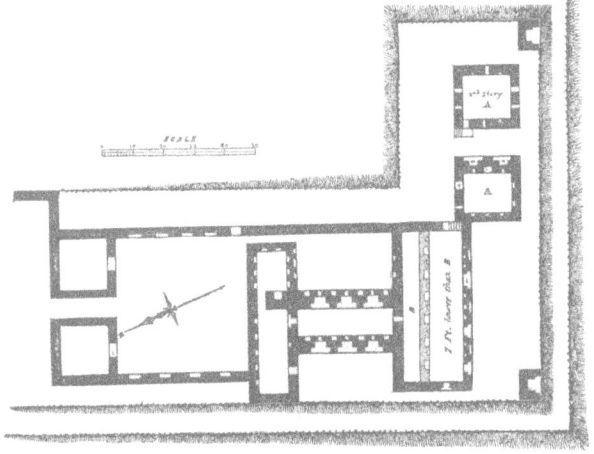

Plan of Palace of Ollantay

Cusi-Coyllur, the Joyful Star, was the daughter of the Inca I'achacutic. Ollantay was a brave and handsome chieftain of the Inca's army, who had carried the Inca power further down toward the Amazonian plains than any of the Inca generals. But he was not of royal blood. Returning in triumph to Cuzco, he was received with unprecedented honors in the Huacapata; but in the very hour when his fame was highest and his ambition most elated, he caught sight of "the Joyful Star," and became the prey of a passion guilty alike in the eyes of religion and the law. None but Incas could ally themselves with those of Inca lineage, and whoever outside of the royal line should aspire to such distinction was adjudged guilty of sacrilege, and visited with the severest of punishment.

I scarcely need tell the rest of it—the old, old story. Thwarted in his suit ignominiously, where any one less distinguished would have been slain, the young chieftain, mad with disappointment and burning with revenge, returns to his army, and in passionate words recounts his wrongs, and asks his soldiers to assist in avenging them. In flying from the capital, however, he pauses on the heights above it, and exclaims:

"Ah, Cuzco! ah, beautiful city!
Thou art filled with my enemies.
Thy perverse bosom will I tear;
Thy heart give to the condors!
Ah, haughty enemy ah, proud Inca!
I will seek the ranks of mine Antis;
I will review my victorious soldiers;
I will give them arrows!
And when on the heights of Sacsahuaman
My men shall gather like a cloud;
There shall they light a flame,
Thence shall descend as a torrent!
Thou shalt fall at my feet, proud Inca
You will ask me, take my daughter,
On my knees I implore my life!"

The army responds to his fiery appeals and hails him Inca. He places on his own head the imperial scarlet Ilautu, And marches on Cuzco. Midway, however, he hears of the approach of the old, astute, and invincible Inca General Rumiñani, whose name of "Stony-Eye" fairly indicates his cold, implacable character. Ollantay, impetuous, but cautious, does not undervalue his powerful and wary antagonist, but seizes on the important position destined to bear his name in future times, fortifies himself, and establishes a firm base for his operations against his sovereign. For ten years he maintains himself here, until, by a wonderful act of treachery, he is made prisoner, and brought to Cuzco to suffer death. But meantime the stern old Inca has died, and his son, whose younger heart can better appreciate the tender passion, touched by the rebel warrior's story, not only pardons him but consents to his marriage with "the Joyful Star," who had all this time been confined in the Aclla-huasi, or Convent of the Vestals. And they lived to a good old age, and were as happy and prolific as the hero and heroine of any modern novel.

And such, according to the old Quichua drama, was the origin of Ollantaytambo. The site of Ollantay's palace is not only pointed out, standing on a series of charming terraces overlooking the smiling valley, but its remains are still distinct, and some parts of it almost entire. It was elaborate in plan, as the reader will see; and it shows also that Inca architecture did not, as has been alleged, balk at the task of raising buildings of more than a single story.

View of Part of Palace of Ollantay

Apropos of the drama of Ollantay, I may add that the Quichua language is one of remarkable beauty and scope, plaintive and soft to the ear. As the language of the Incas it was spread wherever they carried their arms from Quito to Chile, and is still the ruling tongue of the Sierra. As an example, I subjoin a Harvest Song from the drama referred to, with Mr. Markham's translation. It is addressed to the mischievous little black and yellow tuya, a bird that robs the corn fields.

QUICHUA.

Ama pisco micuychu
Ñustallipa chacranta
Manan hina tucuichu
Hillacunan saranta.
Tuyallay! Tuyallay!
Panaccaymi rurumi

Ancha cconi munispa
Nucmunaccmi uccumi
Llullunacmi raphinpa
Tuyallay! Tuyallay !
Phurantatac mascariy
Cuchusaccmi silluta
Puppasccayquin ccantapa
Happiscayquin ccantapas.
Tuyallay! Tuyallay!
Hinasccatan ricunqui
Huc rurunta chapchacctin
Hinac taccmi ricunqui
Huc llallapas chincacctin.
Tuyallay! Tuyallay !
ENGLISH.

O bird, forbear to eat.
The crops of my princess:
Do not thus rob
The maize that is her food!
Tuyallay! Tuyallay!
The fruit is white,
And the leaves are tender,
As yet they are delicate:
I fear your perching on them.
Tuyallay! Tuyallay!
Your wings shall be cut,
Your nails shall be torn,
And you shall be taken
And closely encaged.
Tuyallay! Tuyallay!
This shall be done to you,
When you eat a grain:
This shall be done to you
When a grain is lost.
Tuyallay! Tuyallay!

It was with a pang that I bade farewell forever to Ollantaytambo, equally gardens and fortress, with its climate of endless spring, framed in by the mightiest mountains of our continent, as bare and stern as the valley itself is bright and verdant.

Our return to Urubamba was rapid, and we spent several days there in examining the remains of the palaces and baths of the Incas in and around the picturesque little village of Yucay. Thence up the rich and beautiful valley to the town of Pisac, over which impends the wonderful fortress of the same name.

Almost every step in the valley is marked by monuments of the ancient inhabitants; but I should exhaust the patience of my readers were I to undertake even to enumerate them. I can not omit, however, to notice some remarkable remains near the village of Calca, which illustrate the craft of the Inca priesthood, while giving us a peculiar form of Inca architecture. They occupy that favorite site to which I have had occasion before to allude, the neck of a promontory whence extensive views may be commanded, and over which the roads of a valley like that of Yucay would naturally pass.

The most conspicuous structure is a round building, too low to be called, strictly speaking, a tower. It stands upon a rocky knoll, is twenty-four feet in diameter, and its walls are eighteen feet high to the cornice, which has an exterior projection of ten inches, and an interior one of eight inches. The walls are two feet four inches in thickness at their base. It is built of rough stones, or stones only partly broken into shape, laid in the same tenacious material which I have called clay, and which seems to me to be nothing else. It was originally stuccoed inside and out. The doorway, three feet eight inches wide, opens fifteen degrees west of south; and there are false doors or niches corresponding with it in dimensions at every quadrature of the circle formed by the pan, through each of which opens a small window. Over each of these, as well as over the door, are inverted T's, like the Egyptian Tauco, of which there are also three in each section between the principal niches. These are entirely peculiar to this structure. In the interior, within reach of the hand, and symmetrically distributed, are eight oblong niches, as shown in the plan. The lintels of the doors and niches still remain. They are composed of sticks of wood about the size of a man's arm, closely wound with coarse ropes of pita, or the fibre of the agave, evidently for the purpose of securing an adhesive surface for the smooth coating of stucco that was applied as a finish. This was a common device in buildings of rough stones, concrete, and adobes. We resort substantially to the same thing in our lathing. The height of this structure was probably not much greater than now, and it may be assumed that it was roofed in similar manner with the Sondor-huasi in Azangero.

Its purposes can only be inferred from the character of the adjacent and apparently dependent remains which are both sufficiently singular and suggestive. They are situated sixty feet distant from the tower or circular building, and consist of a number of rectangular structures covering an area of about one hundred feet square, raised around a great limestone boulder, sixty feet long, thirty broad, and twenty-five feet high above the ground. The walls of the buildings come up to the rock and are built against it. Indeed, near the extremities they were carried over it, so as to leave only the ends of the rock exposed. These present their natural surfaces, excepting the northern end, in which is cut a groove or channel of from three to four inches wide, and about three inches deep. This winds around and down the rock in serpentine form for a length of twenty feet, and disappears through one of the transverse walls built against the rock, reappearing in one of the side-buildings or rooms where the rock projects something like the eaves of a house, and there terminates in a kind of spout, carved rudely in the form of a serpent's head. Any liquid poured into the channel at any part would run to this point, and be discharged into whatever vessel might be placed here. That the groove was designed to represent a serpent is obvious from the manner in which it tapers to the tail and widens elsewhere, and from its sinuosities, as well as from its sculptured head.

That isolated rocks were held in great veneration by the ancient Peruvians, were often strangely carved, and frequently had structures of some sort raised around them, and had offerings made to them or the spirit supposed to dwell in them, admits of no dispute. I saw hundreds of such rocks in the country, and to this day there is hardly one at all remarkable for shape or position, on any of the highways of the Sierra to which the Indians do not take off their hats and bow with reverence, uttering in a low voice some words of adjuration. Often this ceremony is accompanied by removing the quid of coca from the mouth and casting it against the rock. Occasionally the Indian searches for a little pebble which he throws against the rock, generally at one point, so that in the course of ages considerable cavities have been worn in the stone by this process.

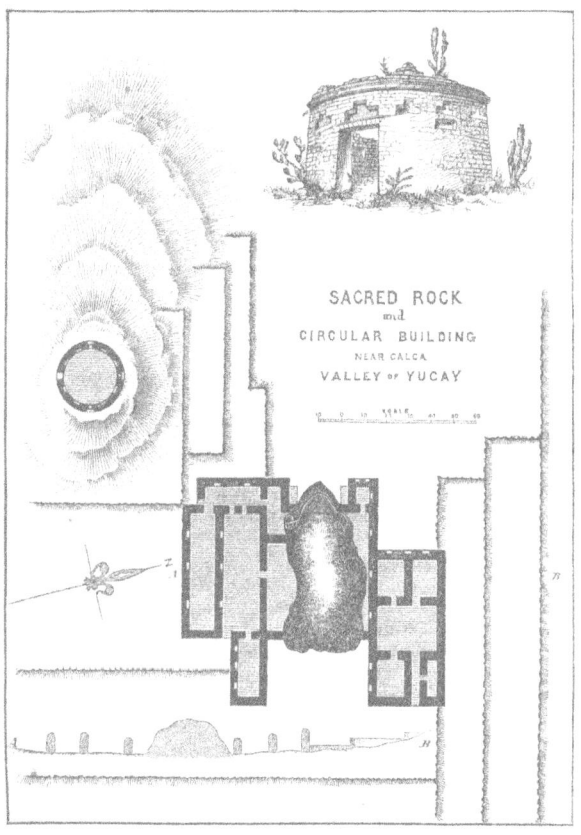

The boulder under notice, from its position and size, is a conspicuous object, and, surrounded as it was by so considerable a pile of edifices, was clearly an object of much sanctity. And as we know sacrifices by libations were common in all parts of Peru, we can readily believe that the serpentine groove around this rock was intended to receive the offerings of chicha that might be made by the travelers obliged to pass this spot in their journeys through the valley. It was cut at a judicious height above the ground, about breast high, so as to facilitate the contributions of the faithful, who probably were never told what became of their offerings after they had flowed away into the recesses of the adjacent buildings to inspire the oracle that spoke to them from the sacred rock. Among the remains of ancient Greece and Rome the antiquarian has often smiled to find the convenient chamber of the priest behind the statues of the dead gods, and the cunningly-devised tubes connecting with their marble lips, through which came words oracular and potent to the trembling questioner who had duly made his offering at their shrines.

I have said that the Incas, with all their power, were unable to extend their empire far to the eastward, or very far down the Amazonian valleys, into the regions of the savage Chunchas or Antis. They stopped short when they reached the thick forests, and at those points raised great fortresses to protect themselves against insult and to resist invasion.

One of the most severely contested of the valleys was that of Paucartambo, lying parallel to that of Yucay, only eight leagues distant, but separated from it by an impassable snowy range of the Andes. Through this range there is but a single pass, formed by the interlocking valleys or rather gorges of two considerable streams, one flowing into the Rio Paucartambo, and the other into the Vilcamayo or Yucay, at a point where stands the town of Pisac. At both ends of this pass were gigantic forts; that dominating Pisac being most formidable, and, taken as a whole, quite as remarkable as that of the Sacsahuaman, and only to be paralleled in the Old World by the great hill forts of India.

Let us imagine a bold headland of mountain, projecting out from the great snowy masses of the Andes, an irregular oval in shape, three miles long, and at its most elevated point 4000 feet high. It is separated by gorge and valley from the parent mountains, except at one point, where it subsides into a relatively low and narrow ridge, scarcely a hundred paces broad. It is rough and forbidding in outline, here running up into splintered peaks, yonder presenting to the valley enormous beetling cliffs, and here and there holding open, level spaces and gentle slopes in its rocky embrace. Except at three points it is absolutely inaccessible. Two of these are on the side toward the Valley of Yucay, which it was mainly designed to defend, and the third is at the narrow neck or ridge connecting it with the parent mountain. Wherever, while in its natural condition it might have been possible for a bold mountaineer to clamber up, there the Incas built up lofty walls of stone against the rock, so as to leave neither foothold nor support for adventurer or assailant. The ascent on the side of the town is by a stairway partly cut in the rock and partly composed of large stones, which winds and zig-zags along the face of the rocky escarpment, in places hanging over dizzy precipices, next turning sharp around projecting bastions of rock, on everyone of which are towers for soldiers, with their magazines of stones ready to be hurled down on an advancing assailant. At long intervals up the laborious ascent, and where some friendly shelf gives room, are resting places — paved or rocky areas, fifteen to twenty feet square, surrounded by stone seats, but always dominated by some sinister, tower, with a doorway opening to its foundation, just within which, or projecting out ominously, you may see the great stone that requires only to be moved a little to crash down upon your head.

At about half-way up the mountain the lower series of cliffs are surmounted, and there are some considerable slopes, which are artificially terraced up with great skill and beauty. These terraces extend to the very edge of the precipices. They are ascended by flights of steps, through the centre of which run narrow couduits, or azequias, down which the water was conducted, not only for irrigating the terraces but to supply the reservoirs connected with the lower series of fortifications. But here also we find every projection or escarpment of rock not only faced up artificially with stones so as to be inaccessible, but crowned with towers, generally round, with openings for looking out, and others through which weapons might be discharged and stones hurled down. On occasional natural shelves, reached in some instances only by stairways, are clusters of buildings, long and narrow, with tall gables, placed close together, with characteristic economy of space. In a word, every rood of surface that can be propped up by terraces and cultivated is carefully dedicated to agriculture; every avenue of ascent, except such as the engineers determined to leave open, is closed, and every commanding and strategic spot is elaborately fortified. There is not a point to the very summit of the first peak of the mountain which is not somewhere commanded or somehow protected by a maze of works that almost defy the skill of the engineer to plan, and which baffle description.

View in the Valley of Yucay from Corridor of the Hacienda Umeres

Between the first and second peaks there is, of course, a depression or saddle—a crest, rather narrow, but so terraced up and leveled as to afford space for a group of structures of beautifully cut stones, and which were undoubtedly religious—for the great mountain fortress of Pisac was almost a province, supporting not only a garrison, but a considerable population. I estimate that the terraces sustaining its andenes, supplied with water by aqueducts carried along the face of the cliffs, through passages excavated in the rock, and artfully from slope to slope of the mountain, would, if extended, roach more than one hundred miles. It had its minor fortifications—forts within forts, its isolated buildings, villages, and, it would appear, its temple, its Inti-huatana, and its priests, warriors, and laborers, and was impregnable and self-sustaining.

The most interesting feature of this group of remains is the Inti-huatani, and as it is best preserved of any of the similar contrivances of Peru—thanks to its almost inaccessible position—I will endeavor to explain it. Etymologically Inti-huatana resolves itself into di, sun, huatana, the place where, or thing with which, anything is tied up. It also signifies a halter. The whole, therefore, is equivalent to "place where the sun is tied up."

These Inti-huatana seem to have always been formed out of a rock, the summit of which was carefully leveled or chiseled away, leaving only in its centre a projection very nearly of the shape and size of a truncated sugar-loaf. That is to say, about ten inches in diameter at base, eight at top, and sixteen inches high. These rocks were not only almost always in conspicuous positions, but also within the courts of temples or buildings plainly religious in origin, or else standing near such structures, within separate inclosures of stone, open to the sky, and clearly such as were never covered by roofs. In this instance the principal bulk and most elevated part of the rock is inclosed by a wall of finely-cut and accurately-fitted stones, resembling in outline the letter D. The rock fills what may be called the curved side of the letter, and here the wall is built close up against it, the inner faces of the stones being cut to fit the irregularities of the rock, while the outer face of the wall is regular and smooth. On this side the wall is about twenty feet high. On the straight side of the letter the wall is prolonged in one direction, and then, becoming lower, bends around on itself so as to form a second and dependent inclosure—an irregular triangle in outline, covering a lower portion of the rock already mentioned. Within this are several interesting features, connected perhaps with the astronomy of the Incas, but which it is not necessary to my purpose to describe.

The entrance to the principal and most elevated inclosure is through a doorway of the usual form, which is reached from the outside by a flight of stone steps. Passing this the explorer finds himself in an irregular, oblong area, with the rock, hewn with some regularity on his right and rising to the level of the outer walls. Steps in the rock lead to its summit, which is cut perfectly smooth and level, affording an area 18 feet long by 16 broad. In the centre of this area, and rising from the living rock, of which it is part, is the Inti-huatana of Pisac. It is in the form of a cone, like a truncated sugar-loaf, sharply cut and perfectly symmetrical, 11 inches in diameter at its base, 9 at its summit, and 16 inches high. I was told by the Gobernador of Pisac, who accompanied me on my visit, that this column, or gnomen, was formerly surrounded by a flat ring of chumpe or Peruvian bronze, several inches wide, which he had often seen when a boy.

Principal Fortress of Ollantaytambo

Of the public, and probably sacred, character of the edifices surrounding the Inti-huatana, there can be no doubt. It is evidenced by their position and peculiarities of structure. Now in all references to the astronomical ideas and achievements of the Incas of Peru we read of certain devices and contrivances by means of which they determined the solstices and equinoxes. We are told by the early chroniclers, Garcillaso de la Vega, Cieza de Leon, Acosta, Betanzos, Sarmiento, Gemelli, and others, that on the eminences around Cuzco and Quito were built what Garcillaso calls towers and Betanzos pyramids, so placed that by noting their shadows, or by taking observations between them, the periods of the solstices and the length of the solar year could be accurately determined. Garcillaso states that at Cuzco there were sixteen of these towers, the largest equal in size to the watch towers of Spain, eight to the east and eight to the west of the city: Acosta says there were twelve; and Betanzos, four. Their site, so far as it is fixed by any of these authorities, was on the hill of Carmenca, dominating Cuzco on the northwest, where Garcillaso states they were standing in 1560. I was unable, however, to find any traces of them on that eminence in 1864.

Besides these solstitial towers, reference is made by the chroniclers to certain single columns or pillars "for determining the equinoxes." These, Garcillaso tell us, were of sculptured stones, richly worked, and placed in the open courts of the Temples of the Sun. It was the duty of the priests, on the approach of the equinox, to watch the shadows of these columns, which were in the centre of circles embracing the whole area of the courts of the temples. Through the centre of each circle (and its column) was drawn a line due east and west. On the day when the centre of the shadow followed this line from sunrise to sunset, and when, at noon, the rays of the sun fell full on the column, and it was "bathed in light," casting no shadow, the priests declared the equinox had arrived, and proceeded to decorate the gnomon with flowers and offerings, placing on it "the Chair of the Sun."

We have here the undoubtedly correct explanation of the purposes of the Inti-huatana of Pisac, which is no doubt a true type of the "columns" of which the chroniclers speak, and through the aid of which they were able to ascertain the periods of the solstices and the arrival of the sun in the zenith.

The Mexicans and Central Americans seem to have made greater advances in astronomy and the computation of time than the Peruvians.

The Inti-Huatana of Pisac.

www.ingramcontent.com/pod-product-compliance
Lightning Source LLC
Chambersburg PA
CBHW070002300526
45794CB00001B/155